Initiative

A course for advanced learners

Teacher's Book

Richard Walton
& Mark Bartram

CAMBRIDGE
UNIVERSITY PRESS

PUBLISHED BY THE PRESS SYNDICATE OF THE UNIVERSITY OF CAMBRIDGE
The Pitt Building, Trumpington Street, Cambridge, United Kingdom

CAMBRIDGE UNIVERSITY PRESS
The Edinburgh Building, Cambridge CB2 2RU, UK   http://www.cup.cam.ac.uk
40 West 20th Street, New York, NY 10011–4211, USA   http://www.cup.org
10 Stamford Road, Oakleigh, Melbourne 3166, Australia
Ruiz de Alarcón 13, 28014 Madrid, Spain

First published 2000

Printed in the United Kingdom at the University Press, Cambridge

Typeface Joanna 10.5pt, Officina Sans 12.5pt *System* QuarkXPress 4.03

ISBN 0 521 57582 6 Student's Book
ISBN 0 521 57581 8 Teacher's Book
ISBN 0 521 57580 X Cassette

Contents

	Introduction	4
Starter Unit		8
Unit 1	Lost for words	14
Unit 2	Healthy mind, healthy body	22
Unit 3	Getting away from it all	28
Unit 4	Crime never pays?	35
Unit 5	You are what you eat	41
Unit 6	Money makes the world go round	48
Unit 7	Back to nature	54
Unit 8	Shop till you drop	60
Unit 9	Lessons in life	67
Unit 10	Read all about it!	72
Unit 11	Living in the city	78
Unit 12	Art for art's sake?	87
Unit 13	What a good idea!	94
Unit 14	Working nine to five	101
Unit 15	It makes you laugh	109
	Communication activities	114

Introduction

Welcome to *Initiative*. We hope you enjoy using the course, and that it enables your students to progress in their English.

Who is the course aimed at?

Initiative is aimed at post upper-intermediate students who are likely to be studying English in full-time education. The course, which consists of a Student's Book, a Teacher's Book and a cassette, is particularly suitable for large groups of tertiary-level students such as those studying at universities. It can also be used with young adults as a general English course in secondary schools and language schools where a serious, study-based approach is preferred.

What are the aims of the course?

- to teach students new language;

- to consolidate existing knowledge;

- to encourage students to explore different ways of thinking about language learning;

- to develop good study habits which can be applied outside the English classroom.

What are the key features of the course?

- the main focus is on the skills of reading and writing, with special attention paid throughout to discourse analysis;

- listening and oral activities are included but are designed to be optional rather than integral to each unit;

- a discovery approach to grammar encourages students to work out rules of usage and structure for themselves;

- there is a strong emphasis on vocabulary and collocation throughout;

- Hearing Perception exercises, which focus intensively on short chunks of language, aim to increase students' ability to understand authentic speech;

- autonomous learning is encouraged by consistent attention to study skills, both within the units and in a special starter unit devoted to this topic.

How long is the course?

- there are 15 theme-based units plus a starter unit;

- each unit is designed to take up between three and four hours of classroom time, providing approximately 48–64 hours of material.

What does the Teacher's Book contain?

- background rationale and general teaching tips on the main sections of the students' material;

- unit by unit notes on the aims and procedures of each section;

- answer keys and tapescripts;

- extra communication activities.

As with any course, the teacher and the students must adapt the coursebook to meet their own needs. The coursebook is only one element of a successful course. We hope you find this one useful and enjoyable.

Richard Walton   Mark Bartram

A guide to the material

To start you thinking

Every unit begins with a short warm-up section which introduces the unit theme and prepares students for the activities which follow.

Reading

The reading texts in *Initiative* have been drawn from a range of authentic sources such as newspapers, magazines, advertisements and literary texts. The following points apply to any text:

- a pre-reading task is provided in most cases. Get students to predict what might be in the text by looking at headlines, subtitles and pictures.

- be aware that students do not necessarily have to understand every word of a text. They may be asked to read quickly to find a piece of information (often called **scanning**), or to summarise the main ideas (**skimming** or **gist reading**). Time limits for scanning and skimming are often suggested in the Student's Book to discourage word-for-word translation.

- some units contain specific tasks on discourse, i.e. the way in which ideas and texts are organised and linked together. These exercises work towards an understanding of how texts are built up as a whole, above the level of the sentence.

- students should have access to a good English-English dictionary which should be used where suggested in the teacher's notes. The *Cambridge International Dictionary of English* (Cambridge University Press, 1995) is recommended.

- where possible, give students the opportunity to compare and discuss answers in a co-operative atmosphere.

Vocabulary and collocation

Vocabulary review is a regular feature of the course, as students need to develop strategies to help them store and remember more lexical items. To help them do so:

- encourage students to process new vocabulary in any of the ways suggested in the coursebook and to store words in a way that has meaning for them;

- tell students that the use of word partnerships (collocations) is the key to successful use of lexis at more advanced levels. Encourage them to adopt some of the suggested ways of storing collocations;

- remind students that, as well as knowing the meaning of a word, they also need to know how to spell and pronounce it, if it has any special grammar features, and if it is restricted to any particular register, for example if it is only used colloquially.

Grammar

The grammar practised in *Initiative* has been selected both to introduce new language and consolidate existing knowledge. The discovery approach to grammar encourages students to 'rediscover' the rules of structure and usage. A typical grammar section draws on the main reading text and provides examples of the chosen structures which students can then recognise from the context.

The Teacher's Book provides a list of anticipated problems for each of the grammar sections, which are highlighted in the Student's Book for easy reference. Students are advised to use a comprehensive reference and practice source such as *Advanced Grammar in Use* by Martin Hewings (Cambridge University Press, 1999).

Listening and pronunciation

The listening texts in *Initiative* are based on authentic recordings from a variety of sources, such as interviews, lectures, local radio advertisements and news bulletins. The following points apply to any listening text:

- a pre-listening task is usually provided, with an additional Focus Task (see box below) suggested in the teacher's notes;

Focus Tasks

Aims

To allow students to listen out for the main points and/or orient themselves with the passage.

Procedure

1 Write suggested questions on the board.

2 Check the students understand them.

3 Play the tape for the first time.

4 Students compare answers in pairs if possible and feed back to the whole class.

- make sure that students read and understand the comprehension questions before they listen, and encourage them to predict what they might hear;

- unless otherwise instructed in the unit notes, tell students that you will play the tape at least twice;

- optional pronunciation exercises often follow the listening texts;

- Hearing Perception activities are included in Units 2, 3, 5, 7, 10, 12 and 13, to improve listening comprehension skills (see box on the right).

Hearing Perception

Aims

While listening comprehension is to do with understanding the message, Hearing Perception aims to raise students' awareness of how authentic English is spoken by focusing intensively on short extracts, and so to help them with both their understanding and their own pronunciation.

Procedure

1 If possible, put students into groups of three and give them three different coloured pens and a sheet of paper. (If group work is not possible, students can do the exercise individually with three coloured pens each.)

2 Tell them they are going to listen **three times** to a short extract, and that they should write down exactly what they hear, even if they don't know what it means. Explain that they should leave a space if they can't make out what is being said and that correct spelling is not important.

3 On the first listening, one of the group writes while the others contribute suggestions. On the second listening, another member of the group makes corrections and additions in a different coloured pen. On the third listening, another member makes any final alterations in a different coloured pen again.

4 Play the extract twice, pausing for 20 seconds after every tone.

5 Play the extract a third time, pausing for 10 seconds only at each tone.

6 Where possible, groups can exchange and compare versions and even correct each other's. You may like to play the extract again without pausing.

7 For the final correct version, ask students to dictate what they have, and you write this on the board with corrections as necessary.

Learner training

This is a key element of *Initiative*, underpinning all sections of the book and specifically in individual activities in the Starter Unit. Students are encouraged to reflect on their learning outside the class, for example, devising a study programme in Unit 3 and finding sources of real English in Unit 13. The following are suggested as general study habits for inside the classroom:

- where possible, students work together, sharing information and knowledge;

- students develop their own study techniques, such as personalised vocabulary stores;

- they are allowed to take risks with their language, for example predicting and making informed guesses;

- students should not be over-corrected, so they feel they have the freedom to experiment. For more ideas and tips on techniques of correcting written English, see *Correction* by Bartram and Walton (Language Teaching Publications, 1991).

Writing

Each unit in *Initiative* has at least one section devoted to writing. The teaching of writing skills is approached in two ways: **product-focused** where students analyse different kinds of texts and imitate them, and **process-focused** where writing is broken down into sub-skills. Detailed instructions are given in the unit notes. Some general tips are:

- where possible, particularly for a process-focused task, students work co-operatively in groups;

- prepare for each writing task with brainstorming activities or discussion;

- make sure students understand the importance of editing and rewriting;

- try to make the correcting process active for the students, for example by asking them to hunt for their own mistakes, devising a correcting code or simply underlining mistakes.

Review

A review section at the end of each unit revises certain language points from the unit before. However, this should form only part of the recycling process, and it is up to the teacher to incorporate other techniques. One such technique is to have a class vocabulary box: you will need an old shoebox, with a slit in the top, through which students 'post' vocabulary items which come up in the lessons. These items form the basis for your regular reviewing.

Communication activities

Each unit in the Teacher's Book contains an optional Communication Activity (linked to the unit theme), for those classes where spoken fluency is important. The procedures and photocopiable worksheets for these activities are in a separate section towards the back of the book (see pages 114–128) and include suggestions as to where they could best be used.

S

Starter Unit

GENERAL INTRODUCTION TO THE STARTER UNIT

The aim of the Starter Unit is to get the students into good study and learning habits right at the beginning of the course. You may find that some of the activities are not appropriate for your particular class. For example, they may have little scope for deciding for themselves what their goals are (section SU.2). If this is the case, feel free to omit them.

However, in most cases, the activities are designed to be useful throughout and beyond the course. For example, students should start recording and classifying vocabulary in the ways suggested (section SU.4) right from the start; equally, being able to use a monolingual dictionary (section SU.7) is a useful skill which will serve them well long after the course has finished.

Two particular language areas are introduced here: collocations (section SU.5) and discourse (section SU.6). Their aim is to encourage students to think about the connections between language items, as well as the items themselves. For instance, when they record a new word, they should also try to record collocations which go with that word.

SU.1 Are you a good language learner?

Aim

To encourage students to think about what good language learning involves.
To lead into the reading passage which follows (and from which the students can get the answers to the questions).

Procedure

Before they open their books, ask the students to brainstorm the factors that make a good language learner. Write these on the board, but don't at this stage pass comment.

a Ask the students to complete the quiz individually or in pairs (perhaps by interviewing each other). You could give them half the questions each.

b The discussion will give students a chance to exchange ideas about habits. Stress that no single person will have the habits of the 'perfect' learner – these are simply habits to aim for.

c The reading passage which follows provides a possible series of 'right' answers, though you should emphasise that these are good habits rather than determining factors. Also that they are opinions, not facts.

It would be worthwhile to discuss with your class the ideas in the quiz and passage, preferably after reading both. The following points could be brought out.

1 Students who have clear, realistic aims will probably do better than those whose aims are rather woolly and/or too ambitious.

2 Students who understand the stages which they must pass through (e.g. from beginner to advanced) will fare better.

3 Practice of new items is vital.

4 A good language learner will be interested in, and try to understand the underlying rules of the language. (This doesn't mean, of course, that students who are not interested in rules will not be able to learn.)

5 Remembering is an essential, but underrated, aspect of language learning.
It is obvious that students who remember more things will speak and understand better. Ways of improving recall are discussed later in this unit.

6 Students checking their own performance (not just in written work) is important. There is much evidence that self-correction/editing is more effective than correction by the teacher.

7 Good language learners tend to seek out native-speakers and make contact with them.

8 All language learners come across difficulties at some stage: these could be linguistic ('I just don't understand the present perfect!') or psychological/ emotional (for example, the so-called 'intermediate plateau'). A good language learner will realise that these difficulties are going to occur, and not get discouraged when they do.

9 Unfortunately, not everybody wants to study English, and not everybody likes it! But it does seem that if you do, you will do better.

10 This is more controversial. Many people believe that English, being more 'international' than other languages, has no particular culture behind it any more. Many people use it, for example, to converse with other non-native speakers. However, it does seem that students who are interested in the background culture will also learn the language better.

> **Key**
>
> According to the ideas in the passage, a perfect language learner would have answered the quiz as follows:
>
> 1 a   2 a   3 e   4 b   5 b, c, d, e   6 a
> 7 b or c   8 a   9 c   10 c or d

SU.2 Setting goals for yourself

Aim

To increase the students' awareness of their own goals and expectations for the course.
To make students realise that all students have different goals.

Procedure

Start by referring back to the reading passage in section SU.1 and especially paragraph two. Pre-teach *goals* and *sub-goals*.

a Stress that this activity must be done individually.

It may be that the students will need some guidance with this activity, perhaps because they have never thought about their own goals before. If you need to give extended guidance, there is a photocopiable worksheet on page 13 of the Teacher's Book. Otherwise, give a couple of examples for each language study area.

Point out that *speaking* does not include pronunciation, which is covered below. Stress that we are talking about goals during the current course, not just at some unspecified point in the future.

The worksheet: sometimes you may have to give possible answers: e.g. for the questions about pronunciation, you could supply two or three choices such as 'I need to be perfect/ comprehensible/ nearly always comprehensible in my pronunciation'.

b Don't let this discussion go on too long – five to ten minutes is enough. Make sure that, by the end, you have got range of goals across the class.

Although each student's aims and needs will be different, it might be worth pointing out the following to the whole class, once the discussion is finished:

1 Reading/listening: when they are reading or listening in their own language, they will hardly ever have to understand or even read/hear every word. Most of the time (especially in reading) they are jumping around, scanning and skimming for information or just to decide what they are going to read, and then only reading in detail the parts they are interested in.

2 Writing/vocabulary: the importance of both these areas depends on what the student needs to do: many do not need to tell stories, or talk about the sounds that animals make. Instead they might need to write reports and talk about machine tools. Each student is different.

3 Grammar: although grammar should not be underestimated, students who have perfect grammar (if such a thing exists) may have to sacrifice other areas of their English. In fact, students like this can sound artificial and stilted. 'Good' grammar means choosing the most effective structure for what you need to say, not just avoiding mistakes.

4 Pronunciation: unless a student actually wants to **sound** like a native English speaker, it is unrealistic and even counterproductive to aim for perfect pronunciation.

5 Generally: different aspects of a student's English progress at different speeds. If they are living in the UK, for example, their listening skills will generally improve faster than, say, their grammar. Also some aspects will **always** progress more slowly – for example, pronunciation and intonation improve more slowly than vocabulary.

SU.3 Devising a programme of work

Aim

To devise a programme of work.

Procedure

a Each student is an individual, and it is unwise for the teacher to try to impose a learning style or programme on the students. However, it is also true that some students find it difficult to make plans and programmes for themselves: for example, they might do no studying during the course, and then review everything at the end, just before the final exam. These students may need help in planning their study.

Ask the students to answer the questions individually at first, then compare with another student. This should provide a fruitful exchange of ideas about learning styles.

b/c Direct your students' attention to the example programme: point out that it is only designed to present a sample to the students. Try to provoke discussion if you can. Then ask students to work out a plan for themselves. This plan should be kept in a safe place by the students – refer back to it at regular intervals during the course, to check that they are keeping to it!

(SU.4) Recording and remembering vocabulary

Aim

To raise the students' awareness of the importance of recording and remembering vocabulary.
To suggest some ways of doing this.

Procedure

a Give the students a few minutes to discuss the graph and then get open-class feedback. The graph shows how the amount of vocabulary learners retain plummets over short periods of time.

Here are some key ideas:

- vocabulary is easier to remember when the students are interested in it;
- vocabulary needs to be processed, i.e. we have to do things mentally with the vocabulary to remember it;
- students need to have some kind of notebook where they can store the new vocabulary, and especially the vocabulary that they **want** to learn;
- vocabulary should be **organised** in some way;
- vocabulary can be remembered more easily by:
  - using visual images
  - making associations
  - activating the new information
  - regular self-testing

- the meaning of a word is not the only thing the students should know about a word. They should also know:
  - how to **pronounce** it;
  - which other words it usually **collocates** with (i.e. you should teach not just the words in isolation, but also common word partners or phrases);
  - if it has any special **grammatical features**, e.g. irregular verbs, verbs followed by -ing, etc.

b Start by asking your students how they keep a record of the vocabulary they want to remember and ask them how successful they think their methods are. Also ask them what things they find easy to remember. The discussion should produce interesting ideas.

c With all these activities, ask students to work first individually, then compare in pairs or groups and finally get some open-class feedback to check various possibilities, particularly where there are suggested answers only.

d If you are short of time, set this story as a homework activity.

> ### Key
>
> **c** 1 (suggested answer shown on previous page)
>
> 2 pick=choose; answer=reply; crazy=nuts; poorly=ill; wealthy≠hard-up; blunt≠sharp; slim≠chubby; costly≠cheap

---

SU.5 The importance of collocation

Aim

To raise the students' awareness of collocation.

Procedure

Write this example sentence on the board and ask your students to comment on it:

Given the evidence, it was the only conclusion we could make.

They will probably reply that *make* 'sounds a bit funny'. Point out that the sentence makes sense and yet a native English speaker would be aware that there is something not quite right about it. In fact, we do not *make a conclusion* in English but *come to* or *draw* or *arrive at a conclusion*. You could say that this is something a native speaker knows through having heard such word partnerships in phrases in context over many years. Many learners of English, on the other hand, are unaware of such collocations.

a Ask the students to do the activity alone and then compare and discuss in pairs when they have finished.

b This exercise can be done in pairs and small groups.

c The exercise uses 10 of the 18 collocations. A follow-up activity (or homework) might be to ask students to write similar sentences using the missing eight. They could even write them with the collocations blanked out, and the other students have to fill in the blanks.

> ### Key
>
> **a** 1 Wrong – you **draw** the curtains
> 2 Right   3 Wrong – you are immaculately **dressed**   4 Wrong – you bleed **profusely**   5 Right
> 6 Wrong – you decide **on** something
> 7 Wrong – you are **fast** asleep
> 8 Wrong – thunder **rumbles**
> 9 Right – or you can also say delighted **by** or **with**   10 Wrong – you **kill** time
>
> **b** 2 verb + adverb   3 verb + noun
> 4 adverb + adjective   5 adjective + noun
> 6 adjective + adjective   7 noun + verb
> 8 verb + preposition
> 9 noun + adjective   10 adjective + noun
> 11 adjective + adjective
> 12 adverb + adjective   13 verb + adverb
> 14 adjective + preposition
> 15 verb + noun   16 noun + adjective
> 17 verb + preposition   18 noun + verb
>
> **c** 2 breathe deeply   3 a spare tyre
> 4 wide awake   5 schools break up
> 6 tell the truth   7 quietly confident
> 8 narrow escape   9 made a mistake
> 10 deadly serious

SU.6 The importance of discourse

Aim

To show students how texts/sentences are linked together in various ways.

Procedure

Start by writing on the board two sentences which have a clear connection between them:

Margaret Thatcher was elected in 1979.
She was Britain's first woman Prime Minister.

Ask the students whether the two sentences are connected, and how (by the word *She*).

Then put up two completely unconnected sentences:

Computers halve in price every eighteen months. My parrot is called Toby.

Elicit the idea that although each sentence on its own makes sense, once you put them together they cease to mean anything.

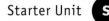

Finally, put up two sentences which have a connection, but one which is implied rather than overt:

The temperature was falling. We closed the windows.

Elicit the idea that the second action is a result of the first, although there is no word such as **so** to show this connection. Explain or elicit that understanding connections between sentences is important both for reading and writing and that these connections are expressed sometimes through special linking words and sometimes through the ideas or content.

a Ask the students to work in pairs or groups to put the text in order. The important thing is that they become aware of the possibilities that are thrown up by the jumbled text. Make sure therefore that you monitor carefully, guiding students who are in difficulty, perhaps by leading questions such as 'What do you think this word refers to?'

b It is very important that you correct the activity, and especially the discussion of the underlined words, with the **whole** class. In this way, the weaker students can start to understand the process.

You should accept answers that are sensible and logical even if they are not the same as the key below (for example, 9 could easily follow 12). Discussion and justification of these alternative answers is often fruitful.

You might like to round off the exercise by listing/eliciting from the students the five main ways in which this text is held together:

- discourse markers such as *firstly*, *finally*, *to sum up*;
- referring words (pronouns like *it* and demonstratives like *these*);
- lexical items which are variations on previous items (e.g. *order* for *tidy*);
- conjunctions like *and*;
- the ideas running through the piece, e.g. the word *answer* refers back to the question posed in the first sentence.

Key

a (suggested order) 1, 13, 11, 3, 6, 12, 4, 2, 7, 10, 9, 5, 8

b Underlined words

   13 *answer* refers back to the first sentence, which asks a question;

   11 *either* shows us that one reason has already been given (and discounted);

   hard work is also being contrasted with *intelligence*;

  3 No, *what seems to count* contrasts with what has gone before;

  6 *these* refers back to *techniques*;

 12 *Firstly* starts the list of techniques;

  4 *For example* introduces an example of orderliness; *order* refers back to *tidy*;

  2 *And* introduces a second example of good organisation;

  7 *In that way* introduces the result of their time-scheduling; *it* refers back to *homework*;

 10 *Secondly* follows on from *Firstly*;

  9 *for instance* introduces an example of *good studying strategies*; the whole content of this box refers to good strategies;

  5 *Finally* introduces the last item in the list;

  8 *To sum up* introduces the conclusion.

SU.7 Choosing a good monolingual dictionary

Aim

To raise students' awareness of the importance of a good monolingual dictionary.
To suggest some criteria by which they might choose one.

Procedure

a Ask students to work in pairs, covering up part b for the moment. When they have finished, spend a few minutes on open-class feedback to see how many of the categories found in the box in part b they managed to come up with.

b Ask students to do this activity individually at first and then to compare answers in pairs/groups.

Key

b 1 pronunciation
   2 word stress (and pronunciation)
   3 alternative spellings
   4 grammatical information
   5 usage
   6 cross-references
   7 collocations
   8 word formation
   9 example sentences
  10 varieties of English

WORKSHEET

Vocabulary:

1 Complete the following sentence:

I need to acquire enough vocabulary to be able to

....

....

....

.... (do what?).

2 Often you need to be able to *understand* more vocabulary than you can actually *use*. In which areas (e.g. medicine, art, history) is this true for you?

Reading:

1 What do you *need* to read in English?

2 What would you *like* to be able to read in English?

3 How much of what you read do you need to understand? Every word?

Writing:

1 What do you *need* to be able to write in English?

2 How good does your writing need to be? Perfect? Comprehensible?

Listening:

1 Which of the following do you need to be able to understand in English? (tick as many as you like):
   ● radio or TV programmes in English
   ● meetings conducted in English
   ● native-speakers when they talk to me
   ● non-native-speakers when they talk to me in English
   ● telephone calls in English
   ● conversations between two native-speakers
   ● other (please specify)

   ....

2 For each of the ones you ticked, say how much you need to understand:
   ● every word
   ● most but not all
   ● the general idea

Grammar:

How good does your grammar *need* to be? Perfect?

Speaking:

Complete the following sentence:

My speaking needs to be good enough to

....

....

....

.... (do what?).

Pronunciation:

1 How good does your pronunciation *need* to be?

2 How good would you like your pronunciation to be?

1

Lost for words

To start you thinking

Aim

To introduce students to the theme of the unit and to suggest a way of categorising vocabulary to make it easier to remember.

Procedure

a Ask students to give you words in their own language whose sound they like. If you have a monolingual class, ask them to vote for the nicest sounding words from a list they or you compile. With a multilingual class, try to find something that all the pleasant-sounding words they suggest have in common.

Now ask students to look at the list of words in the book. Pronounce the words for them but don't say, at this stage, what they mean. Then, individually, students should divide the words into the two categories.

b Students work in pairs to compare. This comparison is important in order to fix the words in their minds. Once again, students should look for similarities in the 'pleasant' words.

c Use monolingual dictionaries for this activity, if possible. The fact that students find the meanings for themselves makes it more likely they will remember the words. Try to ensure that not only the meanings are discovered but also any useful additional information e.g. that *grubby* is an informal word and that *portly* is a humorous word.

Key

c *petal* = the usually brightly coloured parts that form a flower

sloth **1)** (literary) = unwillingness to work or make any effort **2)** South American animal with long arms that moves very slowly and spends most of its time hanging upside down in a tree

conker (British) = the dark brown shiny nut of the horse chestnut tree

---

slime = sticky liquid substance which is unpleasant to touch or the greenish brown substance found near water

miasma (literary) = an unpleasant fog which has a bad smell

grubby (informal) = quite dirty

wriggle = to make small quick movements with the body, turning from side to side

terrapin = type of small North American turtle which lives in warm rivers or lakes

zigzag = (to move in) a line which looks like a row of W's joined together

portly (humorous) = (especially of middle aged or old men) with a fat stomach and chest

fang = a long sharp tooth

yo-yo = a toy which consists of a circular object which can be made to go up and down a long piece of string to which it is tied

---

Reading

Aim

To practise skimming and scanning. (For general points about dealing with reading passages, see the Introduction.)

Procedure

a Explain that the students are going to read three short texts about words. Start by asking what kinds of books or texts might deal with words. (For example, dictionaries, thesauruses, lexicons, books of usage, crossword books, books of word-games and word puzzles, books of poetry criticism, feminist discussions of language, philosophy or linguistic texts, magazine articles discussing new words, or words which the writer dislikes.) Ask how these texts might differ from each other in terms of style and language – any kind of answer which shows the students can think about language should be applauded. It is not important that they make detailed remarks.

Ask them to read through the texts quickly, and answer the three questions in the Student's Book. For all four parts a – d, the students could answer the questions orally in pairs or groups, or, alternatively, jot the answers down quickly in their notebooks.

b This involves a slightly more detailed reading, but continue to encourage students to read reasonably quickly. You might give them a time limit.

Do not answer questions about vocabulary, because firstly this will distract them from the task and secondly you want to encourage the idea that they can do many exercises without understanding everything.

c In this activity, students are asked to look for textual clues and signs in order to identify the text type. The correct answer is not so vital as the process of looking for it: for this reason, the discussion of the answers that you have in full class (when you are correcting the exercise) is very important, as it helps the weaker readers to see what the better readers are doing.

d The final task asks the students to read in more detail.

Key

a 1 Text 3 2 Text 1 3 Text 2

b 1 two 2 (suggested answer) the creativity of human beings 3 babies start to join words together meaningfully 4 the sound of words 5 Joseph Heller

c 1 a manual about bringing up children
2 an introduction to a book
3 a book about new words

d 1 *all gone* is a fixed phrase, whereas *Daddy come* is two words joined together
2 all kinds 3 a situation where something in the situation stops you escaping from it (this answer is quite easy to understand but difficult to formulate – in monolingual classes, you should accept answers in the students' first language).

(1.3) ## Vocabulary

Aim

To practise the skill of guessing vocabulary from context when listening to conversation and to help 'fix' expressions in students' memories.

Procedure

a Ask the students to cover up the right hand column and read through the idioms, thinking what they might mean. Then ask them to uncover the right hand side and work in pairs to match the idioms to the definitions.

b Play the tape twice (at least) and ask them to check their answers, still in their pairs. Stress that they do not need to understand every word of the dialogues to be able to do this.

c Put the students in groups of three or four for this task. Do not worry if this involves some use of their first language(s).

Key

2 i 3 f 4 a 5 j 6 d 7 b 8 g 9 h 10 e
NOTE: some dictionaries offer an additional definition of a *dirty word* as an obscene word.

Tapescript

1 **TEACHER 1**: I think it's vital we try and get more computers installed in the school. We can't start the new millennium with just two PCs.

TEACHER 2: Well, I agree, but you know it's the Head who has the final word on things like that.

2 **FRANK**: Debbie, will … will you marry me?

DEBBIE: Look, Frank, you know I think the world of you, and we'll always be friends, and I respect your judgment awfully …

FRANK: In other words, you don't want to marry me.

DEBBIE: But Frank you've got to understand that I want to go on seeing you, but I see our relationship as like brother and sister …

3 (on the telephone)

OFFICE WORKER: Will all this stuff be ready by Tuesday?

COURIER FIRM MAN: Yes, of course. I give you my word.

OFFICE WORKER: You said that about the last delivery, and that was three days late.

4 **CAL**: I'm going to see Mrs Pringle about a pay rise this afternoon.

DONNA: Are you? Well, I warn you, she's in a pretty bad mood today.

CAL: Oh. Look, I know I shouldn't ask you this, but ·… could you put in a good word for me at the Departmental meeting this morning?

DONNA: Why should I do that?

CAL: Well, you know how hard I've been working, putting in long hours, that sort of thing.

DONNA: (slightly irritated) Look, Cal, this is none of my business, you should go and see her yourself.

5   EDWARD: There's a story going round that Douggie's boy has been … arrested.

IAN: Arrested? What for?

EDWARD: They say he was caught forging signatures on company cheques.

IAN: I don't believe a word of it. That boy hasn't got the courage to cross the road on his own, let alone do anything criminal.

6   1ST SPEAKER: Good match, then?

2ND SPEAKER: Hm, I really have to eat my words on that one.

1ST SPEAKER: How do you mean?

2ND SPEAKER: I'd said that Liverpool would win two-nil.

1ST SPEAKER: Yeah? What made you think that?

2ND SPEAKER: Well, they destroyed them when they played them last month.

1ST SPEAKER: And what was the final score?

2ND SPEAKER: One all. Liverpool went out on away goals.

7   (on the telephone)

REP: Thank you very much for calling Sun Life Widows Insurance. May I ask you how you heard about us?

CUSTOMER: Word of mouth – a friend of mine told me about you, so I thought I'd give you a ring.

REP: And we're very glad you did. Now if there's any more information you'd like …

8   RADIO VOICE:
Attitudes to the whole field of advertising have changed enormously over the past few years. Up until, say, 20 years ago, 'advertising' had always been a dirty word in Britain. It was associated with a rather American approach to the world of business. But that's all changed now – advertising is seen as a dynamic, fashionable area to be in – especially if you call it 'marketing'.

9   1ST MAN: Don't you think that Weaver's been working a bit too hard lately? He's always here until well past six o'clock, and I know he takes work home with him. I'm worried about his health.

2ND MAN: I'll have a word in his ear. No need to tell the whole world.

10   ARTIST: Well, there it is. Five years of work. What do you think?

WOMAN: It's … it's … I'm lost for words, Arturo, I really am.

ARTIST: What do you think about the blue patch in the corner? It's a symbol of freedom, you see. Freedom of the spirit.

WOMAN: Five years, did you say? That long?

(1.4) Grammar – articles

Aim

This section gets students to interact with rules by drawing on knowledge they already have in order to consolidate and extend it. As articles are both notoriously complex and irregular, students' knowledge is likely to be based on experience and not easily expressed in words. With difficult areas of grammar like articles, developing a 'feel' is often more effective than trying to work from rules alone.

Anticipated problems

There are many rules, details and irregularities relating to articles, and this tends to make many students very nervous of them. It's important to encourage a positive attitude so that students do not avoid studying articles, and trying to use them appropriately.

Problems with articles rarely cause serious misunderstanding. At advanced levels, however, subtle shades of meaning and style become increasingly important, and articles are important in this respect.

Inaccuracies generally reflect differences between English and the student's own language.

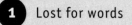

European languages which are broadly similar to English will produce less severe difficulties than others such as Arabic or Japanese, which do not have articles. Teachers are advised to check on such differences as a guide to probable dangers to look out for.

Procedure

Begin by revising the terms *definite*, *indefinite* and *zero* article.

Put students in pairs or groups to brainstorm what influences the choice of articles. Monitor and guide students towards countable, uncountable, general and specific/particular as important concepts.

Elicit these and put them on the board, but don't start discussing rules at this stage.

a This could be done in pairs. Help students to work with their intuition by asking questions like *What have you usually heard/read? What feels, looks, sounds right?*

Don't check the answers yet. Tell the students to wait and that you will come back to this exercise and check the answers later (after part c).

b Ask students to work together in pairs. Monitor closely and point out if they have made a wrong choice, but don't give them the answer.

Check the answers as a whole class.

c Remind students that the examples from part a can go with more than one rule. Encourage them to review their answers to part a, and change their mind if they wish.

As a class, check the answers to both parts a and c together.

d Ask students to work together in pairs, explaining the reasons for their choices. Monitor closely, pointing out the relevant information and giving clues where necessary.

Check the answers as a whole class.

Key

a 1 the   2 a   3 the (ZERO)   4 the
5 a   6 the   7 the   8 a   9 ZERO
10 the   11 ZERO   12 ZERO

b A singular, countable   B Unless
C Plural, uncountable   D first, unknown
E again   F unique   G specific
H general   I any
J musical instrument   K places

c A 2, 3, 4, 5, 6, 8, 10, 12
B 2, 8 (5 may look like an example of
B but it isn't – the information given about
which modern languages this ancient
language becomes makes it specific.)
C 1, 9, 11
D 5 (Also 2: it is unclear at this stage
how the text will progress, and it is
possible that the language may be
specified later, or referred to in some
other way using the definite article.)
E 7
F 4 (Superlatives are unique definition.)
6, 10 (The first word is unique.)
G 1 (Also 10 in that first provides
information specifying the noun.)
H 9, 11
I 2, 8

J 3 (In modern English the zero
article is also used in these cases.)
K 12

d How many words does **an** English speaker know? This is **a** difficult question to answer. For one thing, **the** total will vary from one person to another: it is obvious that **a** scientist will probably know many more words – especially ~~the~~ technical terms – than **a** road sweeper.

There was, for example, **a** story in **the** media recently saying that someone who has just left ~~the~~ school 'knows' 10–12,000 words, but it was clear that **the** story was not based on research.

Furthermore, what do we mean by 'knowing a word?' ~~The~~ People are able to recognise far more words than they actually use – so do you count the words they recognise or the words they use?

(1.5) Conjunctions

Aim

To revise and extend the students' knowledge of conjunctions beyond the basic forms (*so*, *but*, *and*).

Procedure

The three examples from the texts in 1.2 demonstrate two of the five most common functions that are listed later in the section (*contrast*, *contrast* and *result* respectively). Ask students to read quickly through the texts in 1.2 again and underline or highlight any conjunctions they find. With a good class, you could ask students to identify the functions of the conjunctions they find. Run through the five different functions with the students, giving example sentences where necessary.

a Students should complete the task individually and then compare and discuss answers in pairs. Before they start, stress that they need to focus not only on the meaning of the conjunctions but also the sentence forms which come before and after each one. This can be seen in the grammatical constructions, but also in the punctuation. Students should therefore keep an eye on full stops and capital letters. Check answers through open-class feedback.

b Put students in pairs for this task. Check answers through open-class feedback.

c Put students in pairs or small groups to pool ideas. Check answers through open-class feedback.

d Students should complete the task individually and then compare and discuss answers in pairs. Check answers through open-class feedback. If you feel your students are capable, ask them to write whole sentences for themselves to illustrate the use of the ten conjunctions.

Key

a and **b**

1 He passed the examination although he had not studied very hard. (*contrast*)

2 The book was easy to understand despite being written in a strange dialect. (*contrast*)

3 English has very few verb forms whereas some other languages have hundreds! (*contrast*)

4 He decided to learn Russian in order to get a job in Siberia. (*purpose*)

5 She has a teaching qualification as well as speaking three languages. (*extra information*)

6 English has always been receptive to words from other languages and as a result it is full of French and German and Indian vocabulary. (*consequence*)

7 A good dictionary will, of course, provide clear definitions of words. In addition, it should give grammatical information about them. (*extra information*)

8 Many people take intensive language courses at home. However, when they first visit the country where the language is spoken, they find they cannot understand a word! (*contrast*)

9 In many British towns you will find a thriving cultural mix because of the large numbers of ethnic minorities living there. (*reason*)

10 It has become commonplace to avoid certain expressions such as 'mentally handicapped' so as not to offend disadvantaged groups and minorities. (*purpose*)

c (suggested answers)

1 even though, though, despite/in spite of the fact that but **not** even if

2 in spite of

3 while

4 to get, so as to get, so that he could get

5 in addition to

6 consequently, therefore, hence, thus (*last three rather formal/archaic*)

7 Furthermore, Moreover, Also, What's more

8 Yet

9 as a result of, due to, owing to

10 in order not to but **not** not to

d (suggested answers)

1 … France is a republic.
2 … a swimming pool and two tennis courts.
3 … I found it a bit cold.   4 … there was serious flooding.   5 … the traffic.
6 … damage them.   7 … there have been several complaints about your punctuality.
8 … my brother was Olympic High Jump Champion three consecutive times.
9 … be closer to her ageing parents.
10 … the pollution was really bad.

1.6 Learner training

Aim

To introduce to the students the idea of storing vocabulary in memorable and interesting ways. To suggest some ways they might like to do it (but not to impose a storage system on students).

Procedure

a Start with a brief discussion about how the students record new vocabulary they have learnt. In particular, ask them what things they find **easy** to remember, and try to initiate a discussion about how memory works. Some of the ideas you and they might come up with are:

- you remember things more if you are interested in them;
- selecting and organising vocabulary is important;
- using visual imagery and making associations are both useful memorising techniques;
- using the new words actively helps you to recall them;
- regular reviews and self-testing are vital.

Finally, it is worth eliciting or pointing out that when they record a new word, they should also note down:

- the pronunciation
- what other words it collocates with
- if it has any special grammatical features.

When you come to the activities themselves, work through them at a brisk pace.

b The important aspect of this part is that students start their own, **individualised**, word-store. For this reason, it may be better to do this part for homework or, at least, working individually in class.

On the other hand, make sure the students at least try some of the techniques suggested, if only to confirm that they do not like them!

Students should be asked to collect together a sample (as large as possible) of vocabulary items they have studied recently, and use diagrams, lists and charts to store them in ways that are likely to be memorable to the individual student.

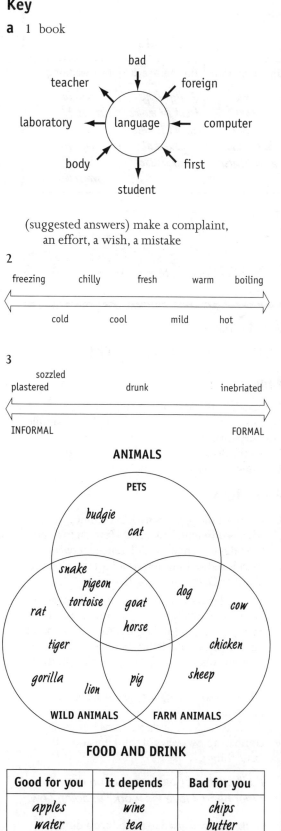

Key

a 1 book

(suggested answers) make a complaint, an effort, a wish, a mistake

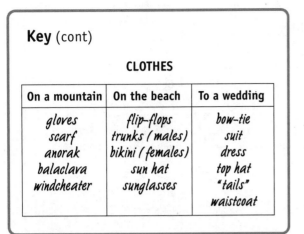

Key (cont)

CLOTHES

On a mountain	On the beach	To a wedding
gloves	flip-flops	bow-tie
scarf	trunks (males)	suit
anorak	bikini (females)	dress
balaclava	sun hat	top hat
windcheater	sunglasses	"tails"
		waistcoat

EXTRA COMMUNICATION ACTIVITY MAY BE DONE HERE *(see page 114)*

1.7 Writing – using discourse markers

Aim

To introduce the idea of signalling the organisation of your writing through very simple discourse markers.
To use the discourse markers in freer writing.
To review earlier work in the unit.

Procedure

a Ask what the pictures have in common, and what is different. This should lead on to a very brief discussion of the differences between speech and writing. You could list these on the board or OHP if you have time.

The students should read through the whole piece individually before starting, in pairs or small groups, to fill the gaps. You should point out that the capital letters have been removed from the discourse markers to make guessing more difficult!

NB: with some language groups, there is a potential confusion between *on the other hand* and *on the contrary*. On the other hand is used when comparing two ways of thinking about the same thing:

I'd like a better paid job, but on the other hand, I love the work I'm doing now.

On the contrary is used to introduce a direct contradiction of what has been said before:

A: I suppose you have an easy life now?
B: On the contrary, I'm busier than ever!

b Ask the students to work through these questions in pairs. Then discuss the answers with the whole class.

c We have chosen a topic here which reviews earlier work in the unit, but any topic is suitable so long as the students are able to think of three or more basic points, with at least one example for each point. Two more suggestions are:

1 Write a piece saying why you like/dislike your country.

2 Write a piece about the problems facing your country.

In both cases, ask the students to set out the text as follows:

(*My country faces a number of problems.*)

Firstly, ...

For example, ...

Secondly ...

An example of this is ...

Finally ...

For instance ...

To sum up ... and as we have said above ...

But make sure the subject matter will not cause political problems in the class.

If you are short of time, you can set this section for homework. Before the students hand it in, make sure that they check the text carefully for mistakes. This should be done in class, at least the first time.

For a discussion of the correction of written work, see the Introduction.

Key

a 2 For example/For instance
3 On the other hand   4 Secondly
5 For example/For instance   6 Finally
7 An example of this   8 To sum up
9 as we said above

b 1 Firstly, Secondly, Finally
2 For example/For instance/An example of this   3 On the other hand
4 as we said above   5 To sum up
6 (suggested answer) to make the organisation and line of thought much easier to follow.

1.8 Writing – punctuation

Aim

To introduce the idea of checking work before handing it in.
To diagnose whether further work on punctuation is needed.

Procedure

Students should correct the text individually, and then compare their answers in pairs, before feeding back to the whole class.

Key

The man generally credited with inventing the crossword puzzle was a journalist named Arthur Wynne, who emigrated to New York from Liverpool. His first crossword appeared in a Sunday newspaper, the 'New York World', on 21 December 1913. Wynne called it a 'word-cross'. The puzzle had the word 'fun' near the top because it appeared on the fun page of the newspaper. The shape resembled a word diamond but the across words differed from the down words.

Readers expressed their approval of the experiment so Wynne devised further puzzles for the paper. By the middle of January, the name had changed from 'word-cross' to 'crossword'. Readers began to contribute their own crosswords.

1.9 Pronunciation – word stress

Aim

To highlight the communicative importance of word stress and to help students develop a better 'ear' for it.

Procedure

a This is an open class activity. Write the word **photograph** on the board and elicit from the students how many syllables it has (3). Then elicit which syllable is pronounced more strongly or loudly than the others, i.e. carries the main stress. Then draw stress bubbles over the word like this:

O o o
photograph

The bubbles show not only where the main stress is but also how many of the syllables are actually pronounced. Go through the same process for **photographer** and **photographic**.

b Students do this task individually and then compare answers in pairs or small groups. Do not give answers at this stage.

c Play the tape, stopping after each word to allow students to check their answers. Use open-class feedback to check answers after each word.

d Put students in pairs for this task and make sure students understand that first A reads out the words with correct stress and B marks the stress with bubbles and then when A has finished their list, B reads out and A marks the stress. Check answers by playing the tape, stopping after each word as above.

Key and tapescript

c

o O o o	O o
photographer	gestures
O o	o o oO o
average	characteristics
o Oo o	o Oo o
apparently	particular
o oO o	oO
situations	delight
O o o	O o o
constantly	dangerous
o O	oO o
applied	existence
o O oo o	ooOo o
alternatively	creativity
o Oo o	O o o
appropriate	frivolous

d

LIST A	LIST B
o Oo o	Oo
humanity	pilot
O o	O o o
language	literature
o O o	o Ooo
expression	associates
o o O o	oO o
entertainment	regarded
o o oO o	o O
communication	excused
o O	o o Oo
request	reproduces
O o	Oo o
business	character
Oo o	oO
lovable	devise
Oo o	O o
animal	jigsaw
o O	o O o
although	enjoyment

2

Healthy mind, healthy body

To start you thinking

Aim

To introduce students to the theme of the unit.

Procedure

a Ask the students to work in pairs using the pictures, spending no more than five minutes.

b Ask students to work in pairs for about ten minutes and then get some open-class feedback. There are no correct answers but you may like to add some interesting facts to the discussion e.g. being married tends to make people (especially men) live longer and suffer less from mental illness; having a pet relaxes you and reduces stress; divorced people (especially men) are much more susceptible to mental illness and have a dramatically increased rate of suicide.

Reading

Aim

To practise skimming articles to get the gist. To distinguish the main point of a passage from subsidiary points.
(For general comments about skimming and other reading skills, see the Introduction.)

Procedure

Start by asking your students which part of the newspaper they read first (you might take a newspaper into class as a piece of realia). Elicit from the students that each person reads a newspaper in a different way, according to their interests etc.

If you can find one, choose a longish article from the paper, and ask the students how they might read it. Elicit that you might read the article very quickly just to see what it is about, if you are interested in it etc. Explain that the skill of skimming, i.e. reading a text in order to discover the general idea (often called its *gist*), is a very useful one, and one that students will often use in their own language.

For both parts a and b, do not allow students to ask you what any words mean or to use dictionaries, as this will only distract them and slow them down. They should be able to do both these tasks without knowing what all the words mean.

a Put the five 'imaginary readers' on the board. After checking your students know what each one does, tell them they have **one minute only** to choose which article(s) would be of interest to each reader. (They should do this individually.)

b Ask students to read through the five topics and skim through the articles to find the correct match. They can do this individually or in pairs. (If you are short of time, combine a and b together.)

c Emphasise that this is not a multiple-choice exercise, in the sense that **all** the points are in the articles.

d Students should do this in small groups. There are no correct answers, but you might like students to vote on the best title produced. The discussion of which title is best might be useful for eliciting the main points of each text.

Key

a a comedian–5; a skin specialist–4; a dietician–3+4; someone worried about not being fit enough–2; a trainee surgeon–1

b 1 Article 4   2 Article 3   3 Article 2
4 Article 1   5 Article 5

c Article 1:2   Article 2:1   Article 3:3
Article 4:3   Article 5:3

d (It is not important for the students to get close to the original titles, but we reproduce them here for interest's sake:
1 Artificial organs.
2 Work-out wonder.
3 Eat, drink and be brainy.
4 Off colour?
5 Laugh your way to better health.)

(2.3) Collocations

Aim

To look at the vocabulary in the articles in greater detail and to extend students' knowledge of collocations related to the unit theme.

Procedure

a Ask students to do the task individually and then check answers in pairs.

b Check that students understand what the first four examples mean. Let them use monolingual dictionaries for the more difficult ones. Check answers around the class.

c Ask students to do the task individually and then check answers in pairs.

Key

a 2 lead 3 oxygenated 4 epidemic
  5 burn off 6 moderate 7 vigorous
  8 counter 9 healing 10 handle 11 at bay
  12 alarming 13 hue 14 twinge
  15 shake off 16 doses 17 on prescription
  18 symptoms

b 1 Medical problems: *side effects; high blood pressure; blood clot*

  2 People who help you with a problem: *stress consultant; General Practitioner*

  3 Treatments: *food supplements; eye test; plastic surgery; flu jab; low-fat diet*

  4 Other: *healthcare; heartbeat; life-support machine; metabolic rate; cancer ward; cholesterol levels*

c 2 side effects 3 on prescription
  4 first aid box 5 shake … off
  6 painkillers 7 metabolic rate
  8 life-support machine 9 twinges
  10 burning off

(2.4) Grammar – review of futures

Aim

This unit reviews both the grammatical forms which can refer to future time, and more importantly checks students' understanding of their meaning – when and why they are used. Although the descriptions of usage given here refer to 'actions', they can also apply equally to states/conditions. Make students aware that not all meanings are covered here, and that they will encounter other uses of these forms. Point out that context is the best guide to interpreting such meanings.

Anticipated problems

- A major aim here is to lead students away from their overuse of *will*, wrongly applied to most contexts.

- The persistent use of the infinitive+time marker in speaking is not uncommon even at quite advanced levels.

- There is often a tendency to miss out the auxiliary *be* in e.g. *she go(es) shopping tomorrow afternoon. *She('s) going to do it.*

- The meaning of many forms depends partly on the mental attitude of the speaker rather than external fact, particularly with: *will; may; might; be going to*+infinitive; Present Continuous.

Note that the distinction between the usage and meaning of some forms is not always black or white and sometimes an English speaker might choose more than one.

Especially:

- *be going to*+infinitive for intentions versus Present Continuous for arrangements. The choice depends how far the plan has been made concrete and in some situations this is a grey area where either form may be used.

- *will* versus *be going to*+infinitive for predictions. Where the action is clearly just about to happen, we generally don't use *will*, but where the certainty of the prediction is based on other evidence the choice is not so fixed. In weather reports, for instance, either are often used with little or no difference in meaning.

- *might* generally suggests lower probability than *may*, but the degree of probability indicated by these can vary according to context and intonation.

Procedure

- In order to activate in the students' minds the many future forms they have met before, begin by asking them how many there are in English. You could brainstorm this individually or in pairs.

- Put the forms they suggest on the board, but delay answering any queries until later, after part b.

a Ask students to work individually.

Then remind them that will is not used as often as many students think, and ask them to compare their answers with a partner. Tell them to explain their answers to each other if they disagree.

Check the answers as a whole class. If students have any questions, ask them if they can find the answers to them for themselves in the next exercise.

b Ask students to work in pairs or in threes so that they can help each other. Monitor closely giving help, but don't tell them the correct answers. If they've got one wrong and it is interfering with further choices, it's helpful to tell them which answers are wrong.

Check the answers as a whole class and answer any queries on form or meaning.

c Ask students to work individually.

Then ask them to compare their answers with a partner. Tell them to explain their answers to each other by referring back to the uses in part b if they disagree.

Check the answers as a whole class.

Key

a
1. 's meeting ('s going to meet)
2. starts
3. are you going to write about
4. might (may)
5. might (may)
6. ✓
7. 'm going to ask
8. ✓

b
2. might/may+infinitive without 'to'-g
3. Present Simple-e
4. be going to +infinitive-f
5. will +infinitive without 'to'-h
6. be going to +infinitive-k
7. Future Continuous-b
8. Future Perfect Simple-a
9. Future Perfect Continuous-c
10. will +infinitive without 'to'
11. Future Continuous-j
12. might/may+infinitive without 'to'-i

c
1. 's going to be
2. 'm meeting
3. 'll be working
4. does … start
5. 'll have had
6. starts; 're going to be
7. won't be
8. will have been working
9. may/might try; may/might visit
10. may/might prove
11. 'll be thinking; 're having
12. 'll phone

2.5 Listening

Aim

To understand the main points of a listening passage from an authentic source.

Procedure

a The students should discuss the questions in pairs. Use the visuals to aid discussion if you feel this would help. Then feed back to the whole class – the discussion which comes out of this feedback should help the students to prepare for the listening.

b You may like to include a Focus Task (see Introduction page 6.)

Suggested Focus Task:

F Write down a total of ten words and phrases that you expect to hear in the passage. Whilst listening for the first time, tick which of the words and phrases came up.

When you move on to the questions in the Student's Book, make sure the students read them **before** they listen to the cassette. Check there are no problems with vocabulary in the questions.

Play the tape at least twice. If circumstances permit, you might like to ask students how many times they want to listen.

Students should check their answers in pairs before feeding back to the whole class.

Key

b 1 About a year ago.
2 Unclear – it may have been intolerance rather than an allergy.
3 Skin tests and blood tests.
4 Antibodies in the blood.
5 (Any three from) milk, eggs, shellfish, fish and peanuts.
6 Migraine, irritable bowel, achy joints, not feeling well, tiredness, Crohn's disease, rheumatoid arthritis, eczema.
7 Bread (wheat and yeast), alcohol (yeast in beer), cheese and butter (both dairy products).
8 With little sympathy – they are often labelled 'neurotic'.

Tapescript

VOICE 1: About a year ago I had a violent reaction to something I ate. 'My first allergy,' I thought. Earlier this century any such reaction was referred to as an allergy, but not now says Dr Jonathon Brostov, physician in charge of the Allergy Clinic at the Middlesex Hospital in London.

VOICE 2: People say that if they're affected by something, they must be allergic, but, strictly speaking, food allergy has a definable immunological response, the reaction is quick – put a peanut on your lip and you swell. Skin tests are positive, blood test is positive and it's really very easy to diagnose because the patient tells you the diagnosis.

VOICE 1: Classical food allergies are clearly detectable by the presence of specific antibodies called IGE in the blood. The most common culprits are milk, eggs, shellfish, fish and peanuts. But there's also a less dramatic reaction to food, what doctors call food intolerance.

VOICE 2: Food intolerance is 'mechanism unknown', although it may be immunological because you do have thirty feet of intestine and it's difficult to know what happens all the way down there. The reactions are much slower, it's usually the 'total load', you eat a lot of a particular food. And the diseases are those perhaps a little bit indeterminate, migraine, irritable bowel, achy joints, 'I don't feel well', 'I'm tired' but also diseases such as Crohn's disease, rheumatoid arthritis, eczema – all affected by food, possibly by immunological mechanisms, possibly not.

VOICE 1: Most often people are intolerant to common foods such as wheat, yeast and dairy products – foods they consume every day, little realising they're aggravating or even causing their symptoms … Orthodox medical opinion is often sceptical about food sensitivities, especially food intolerance. Patients with vague symptoms are easily fobbed off by their GPs and labelled neurotic. They may turn to alternative forms of testing and treatment – hair strand analysis, kinesiology and others, sometimes with effective results, others less so.

2.6 Pronunciation – weak and strong forms

Aim

To help students hear the difference between weak and strong forms, and analyse which parts of a sentence may be expected to be weak or strong.

Procedure

a In pairs, students look at the sentences, trying to agree which are the main verbs and which are auxiliary. They can either devise a way to mark the words in their books or make lists in a notebook.

b Play the tape, stopping after each sentence to allow students to check and discuss their answers. Discuss their conclusions through open-class feedback.

c Students practise saying the sentences while you go round and monitor.

d Students look at the pairs of sentences with their partner and discuss if the auxiliary verb is weak or strong in each case. When they have finished, play the tape, stopping after each pair to allow students to check their answers.

Key

a **MV=main verb, AV=auxiliary verb**

1 MV=seeing, AV='s   2 MV=examined, AV=has   3 MV=have, AV=shall
4 MV=threatening, AV=was
5 MV=find out, AV=could, MV=is
6 MV=injured, AV=were   7 MV=been, AV='ve   8 MV=do (2nd one), AV=do (1st one)   9 MV=believe, AV=did
10 MV=purchase, AV=can

b Main verbs are pronounced with a strong form and auxiliary verbs with a weak form.

d   1 a) weak b) strong   2 a) strong b) weak
   3 a) weak b) strong   4 a) strong b) weak
   5 a) weak b) strong   6 a) weak b) strong
   7 a) strong b) weak   8 a) weak b) strong

Tapescript

b   1 He's been seeing a psychiatrist for two years.
   2 Has the doctor examined you yet?
   3 What shall we have for supper tonight?
   4 It was threatening to become an ugly situation.
   5 If we could only find out what the problem is …
   6 The two climbers were injured.
   7 There've been six or seven similar accidents in the last two years.
   8 What time do they normally do these tests?
   9 Did you really believe him?
   10 Patients can purchase tea and coffee on level four.

d   1 a) Can you help me?
      b) I'm not sure if you can.
   2 a) Oh, I do like geraniums!
      b) Do you think so?
   3 a) How many heart attacks has he had?
      b) Oh yes he has.
   4 a) How do you spell 'could'?
      b) At what time could you get here?
   5 a) What on earth were you thinking of?
      b) Well, we were going to Ibiza, but at the last moment we decided to go to Blackpool instead.
   6 a) Where did you go?
      b) He said he spoke to her, but I don't know if he really did.
   7 a) A: She's living in Manchester now, isn't she?
         B: She was, but she's moved.
      b) There was a man at the bus stop.
   8 a) Where have you been hiding?
      b) Yes, I have.

EXTRA COMMUNICATION ACTIVITY MAY BE DONE HERE *(see page 114)*

 2.7

Hearing perception

Aim and procedure

See Introduction.

Tapescript

(*=tone)

Food intolerance is 'mechanism unknown', *although it may be immunological *because you do have thirty feet of intestine *and it's difficult to know what happens* all the way down there.* The reactions are much slower, *it's usually the 'total load', *you eat a lot of a particular food. *And the diseases are those perhaps a little bit indeterminate, *migraine, irritable bowel, *achy joints, * 'I don't feel well', * 'I'm tired' *but also diseases such as Crohn's disease, *rheumatoid arthritis, eczema *all affected by food, *possibly by immunological mechanisms, possibly not.

2.8

Learner training

Aim

To teach students one way of grouping adjectives according to how appropriate they are in a given context.

Procedure

a Draw the circles on page 31 of the Student's Book on the board and elicit from the class some words that fit in the overlap areas. Ask students, in pairs, to do the same with the other words and phrases in the bubble. Compare answers in a whole class discussion.

b Students now use the words and phrases in their own responses to the ten questions. Tell students it is much more natural to start their answer with qualifying words like *a bit … /rather … /pretty …* (meaning *rather*) or *absolutely …* (if describing an extreme feeling) than just the appropriate adjective.

Key

a mind positive – *chuffed, over the moon, chirpy*
overlap positive – *perky, tip-top*
body positive – *full of beans, in the pink*
mind negative – *on edge, blue, cheesed off, down in the dumps, got at, grumpy*
body negative – *off-colour, run down, under the weather, peaky*

b
1 Pretty chuffed
2 A bit got at/cheesed off
3 Absolutely tip-top/Full of beans
4 A bit run down
5 A bit under the weather/peaky
6 Rather down in the dumps
7 Absolutely dreadful
8 Absolutely over the moon
9 Pretty grumpy/cheesed off
10 Rather on edge

2.9 Writing – brainstorming for ideas

Aim

The aim of this section is to help students brainstorm for ideas, make notes and prepare to write a short article in paragraphs.

Procedure

a You may have to explain that writing down as many ideas about a topic as possible in a limited time (brainstorming) is a good way of beginning a writing project. Look at the notes in class and tell students they have no more than ten minutes to add some more, working in pairs or small groups.

NB: to help students brainstorm, tell them about the *WH … question technique*, which simply means asking oneself questions (*Why? Where? Who? How?* etc.) about the given topic.

b Still in small groups, students arrange ideas into paragraphs. Be ready to help where necessary, encouraging them to discard any bad or irrelevant ideas that came out of the brainstorming.

c Students now write their article, individually in class or for homework.

Key

(suggested answer)

<u>Looking after your health every day</u>

Many people fail to realise that good health is something we can all achieve through establishing good habits and routines in our everyday lives.

One of the most obvious ways we can look after ourselves is by watching what we eat. Fresh fruit and vegetables are musts while junk food is out. Be careful with meat. White meat and

fish are fine but red meat, especially if fried, is very bad for you. Watch out for what you drink as well. Most people drink coffee and tea but caffeine, which is found in both of them, has been shown to be bad for you. A little alcohol is probably quite good for you but drinking too much can be disastrous. Another big no-no is smoking! And yet many people still do it – including teenagers. The only advice here is give up right now.

Of course, physical health is only half the story. You also need to look after your mind. On this front, the main warning is avoid stress as much as possible in today's hectic world. Experts say you should ideally live in the country far from the madding crowd. But if you can't manage that, don't live alone – apparently married people enjoy the best mental health! But don't despair if you haven't got a special friend, try getting a dog or a cat. Stroking a pet relaxes you and helps you unwind.

The great antidote to stress and bad diet is exercise. To be really healthy, you need to take plenty of exercise – especially swimming. But even if you haven't got time for that – how about going to work by bike or even walking. Driving the car means no exercise and a large daily dose of stress!

Anyway, think about it. It's up to you in the end but, as you can see, getting healthy seems fairly easy – it just takes a little will power!

2.10 Review

Aim

To review selected language items from Unit 1.

Procedure

Ask students to do the task individually and then compare answers in pairs. If they have doubts, allow them to refer back to the previous unit. Check answers through open-class feedback.

Key

1 the   2 a   3 put   4 as   5 Although
6 as   7 despite   8 mouth   9 eat
10 however

3

Getting away from it all

3.1 To start you thinking

Aim

To introduce students to the themes of the unit and to review language they already know related to the themes.

Procedure

Give students three minutes to think about their answers to the questions in the Student's Book. Encourage them to take brief notes if they wish. Then put them into groups of three or four and allow them to discuss their own and each other's experiences for as long as you feel is useful. Finally, get some open-class feedback from each group on any interesting points their discussions have thrown up. You may also like to tell students about your own experiences.

3.2 Discussion

Aim

To prepare students for the following reading passages and encourage fluency.

Procedure

a Students do the task individually. Set a time limit of two minutes to avoid too much agonising.

b Put students in groups of three or four. Make sure they understand that the discussion is to find out WHY other people have chosen their three objects; it should not simply be a comparison of lists! Set a time limit of five minutes. Go round and monitor discussions but do not correct unless communication breaks down.

3.3 Reading

Aim

To read for detail. (See Introduction for a general discussion of reading skills.)

Procedure

a Make sure students work alone at this stage.

b First of all, students work in pairs to compare their answers. Then, in open class, the students have to explain the links between the descriptions of the people and the facts and ideas in the short texts.

> **Key**
>
> a Text 1=Person E
> Text 2=Person C
> Text 3=Person D
> Text 4=Person A
> Text 5=Person B

3.4 Reading

Aim

To practise scanning.
To increase the students' awareness of the linking ideas between and within paragraphs.

Procedure

a Remind students that scanning only requires them to answer the questions asked and nothing more. Tell them that they will have a chance to read the text in detail later. Set a time limit of three minutes for the scanning – you can always extend this if necessary. Students should do this part individually.

b Students will need a good deal of time to read the text more carefully in order to understand the relationship of ideas between and within paragraphs. They could do this individually or in pairs, but make sure they have time to compare ideas at some point.

28

When feeding back to the whole class, give ample time for discussion of why particular answers are more likely than others – the aim is to raise awareness of how texts link together, rather than simply to test the students. For one or two of the spaces, more than one answer is possible (see below); be amenable to other answers if the student's justification is a good one.

Key

a 1 A woman (lines 56–58)
2 Britain and specifically London (lines 36–42)
3 Yes (line 37)
4 Her girlfriends (lines 54–58)
5 No (line 71)
6 Wild boar (line 78)
7 Through impersonating a wild boar (lines 90-95)
8 How to order wild boar in Spanish, French and Italian (lines 85–87)

b A2 (*all this* refers to the long preamble at the start of the piece; the paragraph also provides a kind of summary of what has gone before – the *point*.)

B6 (*Years ago* compares with *over the past two years* two paragraphs later.)

C1 (*Promises* refers back to *vowed* in line 54; *however* indicates that the new situation will be in contrast to the promise she made before.)

D3 (*to be honest* is preparing readers for the confession that she doesn't like wild boar herself.) NB: as this is a humorous article, 5 would also be possible – implying that sweethearts always like different things.

E7 (*This* refers back to *my increased knowledge* – indicating that she developed her language capacity in order to stop her sweetheart doing his impersonations.)

F4 (*So* signals a conclusion.)

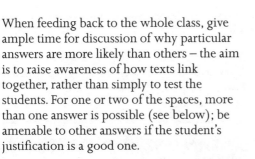

3.5 Vocabulary

Aim

To focus on the skill of guessing unknown vocabulary from context.

Procedure

a Put students in pairs and refer them back to article 3.4, where they will find all the words in context. Tell them they must not use a dictionary but try to arrive at the

(approximate) meaning through contextual clues and logic. Give them a flexible ten minutes for this task.

b If possible, put pairs together to form groups of four to compare and discuss their answers. They must be prepared to explain their answers. Set a time limit of three or four minutes for this.

Key

(suggested answers though similar ideas may be accepted)

1 moving/opening rather secretively 2 low quality 3 (friendly) happiness 4 talking quickly without making much sense
5 pyjamas 6 promised (solemnly) 7 friend
8 all in disorder/mixed up 9 going crazy
10 boy/girlfriend, lover 11 making a noise like a pig 12 smiled with great pleasure

3.6 Reading

Aim

To predict lexical content.
To search for textual clues.

Procedure

Start by drawing the students' attention to the eight locations in the box (or write them on the board). Explain that they are going to read five short articles about five of these places. Ask them to predict a few of the words and names that might come up for each one. Write these on the board.

Then ask students, in pairs if possible, to read through the pieces moderately quickly and match the texts with the places. Point out that they are not expected to be familiar with all of the proper names mentioned – it is not a test of geography.

As a rounding off activity (and if you have time), ask them how many of their predicted words came up.

Key

(textual clues in brackets)

1 China (the Great Wall; Xian; Terracotta Army; River Li; Willow Pattern)

2 India (Moghul area; temples; rice paddies; the Arabian Sea)

3 Greece (ancient ruins; Homer; island ferry; Tinos; Ouzo; Santorini)

4 Costa Rica (Pacific Ocean; Caribbean; Western hemisphere; USA and Canada)
5 New Zealand (rugby; sheep; each island; the north; the south)

Key

2 itchy feet   3 tourist trap   4 travel light
5 day-trippers   6 beaten track   7 hitch-hiked
8 work my passage   9 scenic route
10 bucket shop

3.7 Vocabulary

Aim

To review topic vocabulary and encourage students to use a vocabulary recording technique already presented in this book.

Procedure

Tell the students to copy the arrowed circles into their own vocabulary notebooks and refer them back to the short passages in 3.6, where they will find all the answers. Students do not need to think of any other answers, though you may ask them to suggest other possibilities after you have checked their answers.

Key

1 (*beach*) beautiful, unspoilt, secluded, glorious
2 (*people*) friendly, smiling, charming   3 (*hotel*) charming, local, spotlessly clean, first class, sophisticated   4 (*water/lake/sea*) emerald, placid, blue, crystal clear   5 (*scenery/countryside*) spectacular, breathtaking, rolling, attractive
6 (*experience*) enticing, enigmatic, once-in-a-lifetime, never-to-be-forgotten

---

3.8 Learner training

Aim

To practise using an English-English dictionary to find idioms.
To teach some useful idioms to do with travel.

Procedure

Make sure the students have access to good English-English dictionaries – at least one for every two students. Students should search for the underlined words individually or in pairs and fill the gaps. If your class is suitable, make the exercise into a game whereby the students who finish first receive points. Students then check with the dictionary.

EXTRA COMMUNICATION ACTIVITY MAY BE DONE HERE (*see page 116*)

3.9 Writing – formal letter

Aim

The aim of this section is to write a simple formal letter, concentrating on the layout.

Procedure

a Start by writing (mixed up) twelve or so phrases on the board, half of which are clearly formal in register, and half are clearly informal. Ask the students, working individually, to divide the words into two groups according to any criteria they like. Give them two or three minutes for this. Then ask the students to tell the class how they did it. Usually, at least one student will come up with the informal/formal categorisation. (If they don't, just list the phrases in informal and formal lists, and elicit from the students.)

Suggestions for formal phrases

1 I look forward to hearing from you at your earliest convenience.
2 We regret to inform you that you have not been selected for the post.
3 I shall have no alternative but to cancel the order.
4 As you will see from the enclosed curriculum vitae, I have considerable experience in this field.
5 I am writing in response to your advertisement in yesterday's *Independent*.
6 I hope this matter will receive your prompt attention.

Suggestions for informal phrases

1 Sorry I haven't written for ages but you know how it is!
2 It was great to hear from you again after such a long time.
3 Take care of yourself and keep in touch.
4 Thanks for your postcard from Peru – it looks fantastic!

5 Anyway, do you fancy coming to our garden party on 26th June?

6 I'm afraid we won't be able to make it after all.

Once you have established the idea of formality and informality, you could ask students to list the kinds of formal letter (of complaint, of enquiry etc.), and what kinds of language are inappropriate for a formal letter. (Examples might be: colloquial language, contractions, exclamation marks, friendly register.)

Ask the students to read the twelve components in the Student's Book very quickly and tell you what kind of letter it is. Ask them in pairs to sort it out and write it in their notebooks.

b Check that students have understood what their task is, i.e. using the outline letter as a guide, to produce a formal but polite letter of complaint culminating in a request for a full refund of the cost of the holiday. You may like to run through a possible letter orally, *before* they start writing.

The letter can either be set as homework or done in class. As a guide, students should write between 200 and 250 words in the main body of the letter, i.e. excluding addresses, dates, salutations.

> **Key**
>
> **a** 1 D 2 H 3 E 4 A 5 K 6 G 7 J 8 I
> 9 C 10 B 11 F 12 L
>
> **b** See sample letter below.

32 Ridgeway Road
Bridstow BD5 6XD

15th September

Mr F Bond
Sunspot Holidays
101 Old Road
Bridstow BD1 1HD

Re: Walker - 2-week 'Gold Star Break' 28/8 to 10/9

Dear Mr Bond

I am writing to complain in the strongest possible terms about my 'Gold Star Break' to Rovano in Sileria from 28th August to 10th September.

First of all, the flight out was delayed by two hours. The Sunspot Holidays representative could offer no explanation for the delay and more than thirty people, including small children, were left sitting in the departure lounge in the hot sunshine. Not only this but all our luggage was sent to the wrong airport which meant we did not have a change of clothes for three days. Certainly a very inauspicious start.

On arrival, we discovered that the hotel, described in your brochure as 'the last word in luxury', had not even been finished. Builders were still at work creating a great deal of noise and dirt. Moreover, the hotel staff were decidedly impolite and the food was monotonous. The excursions were extremely poorly organised and two of them had to be cancelled at the last minute, causing further irritation and inconvenience.

As for the resort itself, far from being 'an oasis of calm and beauty', Rovano appears to be a most unattractive, modern town, consisting mainly of cheap souvenir shops, blocks of flats for gullible tourists and terribly noisy all-night discotheques.

Finally, the return flight was also delayed, this time by a staggering eight hours. As before, no explanation was offered.

All in all, this was by any standards a disastrous holiday, which can only reflect badly on your own reputation. My wife and I were, to say the very least, extremely disappointed by the service your agency offered and feel that, under the circumstances, it would not be unreasonable to ask you for a full refund of the cost of our 'holiday'.

I look forward to hearing from you.

Yours sincerely

Lindsay Walker

LINDSAY WALKER

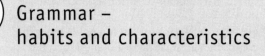

(3.10) Grammar – habits and characteristics

Aim

This section focuses on structures used to talk about habits and characteristics, and has two aims:

- To show how this new meaning can be expressed by familiar structures:
  - Present Continuous
  - Past Continuous
  - *will* + verb
  - *would* + verb
- To show how the structures above differ in meaning from others which students would normally use in this context:
  - *used to* + infinitive
  - Present Simple

Anticipated problems

- Students may have some difficulty understanding the difference between *used to* + infinitive, which is used for both states/conditions and actions, and *would*, which is used only for regular actions. (Although this is generally true, you might warn students that *would* is sometimes used for talking about what appears to be a state/condition, i.e. with stative verbs. Rules on this are not reliable, and students are best advised to avoid it until they learn from experience.)
- Students need to remember that when Present or Past Continuous are used to talk about habits and characteristics, the adverbs *always*, *forever* or *constantly* must be used.

Procedure

Before looking at part a, you could ask students which grammar is used to talk about habits and characteristics in the past and present, giving examples to elicit *used to* + infinitive and *always* + Present Simple.

a Before starting this, you could ask students to look at the text in 3.4 (page 35) again, in pairs, and find other ways of expressing the meaning of the examples, then do the exercise to consolidate.

Alternatively, go straight into the exercise with students working alone before quickly comparing their answers with a neighbour.

If students have queries, refer them to the first part of b to find the answers for themselves.

b Ask students to work together in pairs. Monitor closely giving clues where necessary but not answers.

Check the answers as a whole class, and deal with any problems before moving on to the next part.

c Ask students to work together in pairs, explaining the reasons for their choices. Monitor closely pointing out the relevant information and giving clues where necessary.

Check the answers as a whole class.

Key

a 2 *would* + verb; past
   3 *always* + Present Continuous; general time
   4 *will* + verb; general time

b 1 In sentence 2 in part a, *would* + verb could be replaced by *used to* + infinitive.
   2 a is wrong because *would* + verb is not generally used for talking about states/conditions; *used to* + infinitive is used for states/conditions.
   3 a he was
      b she's always/forever talking
      c used to be

c 1 I'm always forgetting
   2 would get up/used to get up
   3 was always getting/used to get
   4 she'll help
   5 used to have
   6 would bring/used to bring
   7 won't sit
   8 was always asking
   9 would go/used to go
   10 used to think

(3.11) Listening

Aim

To gain the main points from a semi-authentic listening passage.

Procedure

> ### Suggested Focus Task:
>
> Are these statements True or False?
> 1 The reporter is in Greece.
> 2 People in Tarpon Springs behave in a traditionally Greek manner.

(F)

As usual, make sure the students read the questions before you play the cassette. Play the cassette at least twice.

Students should discuss their answers to the questions in pairs and small groups, before feeding back to the whole class.

Key

1 B 2 Route 19 3 No (unattractive) 4 a (big) Greek Orthodox church 5 When he leaves the church and re-enters real America! 6 one in three 7 Because they are the same now as they were when they left Greece in the early 1900s. 8 Boys (in families) 9 It's for men only in modern-day USA. 10 Playing cards and talking to friends (camaraderie).

Tapescript

FEMALE REPORTER: No, that's not the wrong tape. I **am** in Florida. About half an hour's drive northwest of Tampa. I've come up on Route 19, which is about as unattractive an American highway as I've ever seen. But just off that main road is this small old-fashioned town of Tarpon Springs and right in the middle is a big church, which, to my surprise, is Greek Orthodox!

YOUNGER LOCAL MAN: Coming here to Tarpon Springs **is** like having a place you could call Athens with a zip code. It is as if you are in Greece, there are people here after forty years who still speak Greek and know perhaps a few words of English. There are times when you become confused, you step outside of the church after the rituals of incense and worship and prayer and you expect to be on a Greek island and down the street becomes the confusing part when you have um the prefabrication of American shopping malls, etc.

FEMALE REPORTER: One in three of the population here is Greek. I'm standing outside the Parthenon Bakery on Athens Street and inside the locals are speaking Greek amongst themselves and they really seem to revel in all things Greek.

LOCAL WOMAN: I'd say that now our customs are probably more traditional than they are in Greece because the people came here, they had their traditions when they left in the early nineteen hundreds and they never changed. The men get preferential treatment in families; if there are boys, they come first. They're spoiled. Yeah, it's kind of like a time-warp, I guess. Yeah.

OLDER LOCAL MAN: Here on the right we have the Greek traditional coffee shop, men only.

FEMALE REPORTER: Men only in nineteen ninety five in the United States? This doesn't seem possible!

OLDER LOCAL MAN: You('ve) got to remember you're in Tarpon Springs, it's a Greek village and the Greek man, I think you can call him a chauvinist. This is a place for the men to gather and in Tarpon Springs it was where all the sponge divers and all the crews and everyone gathered. You play cards, there's a lot of camaraderie. It's just a place for men only. In nineteen ninety five. Ha ha.

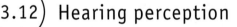

(3.12) # Hearing perception

Aim and procedure

See Introduction.

Tapescript

(*=tone)

Coming here to Tarpon Springs ***is** like having a place you could call *Athens with a zip code. *It is as if you are in Greece, *there are people here after forty years *who still speak Greek and know perhaps a few words of English. *There are times when you become confused, *you step outside of the church *after the rituals of incense and worship and prayer *and you expect to be on a Greek island *and down the street becomes the confusing part when you have um *the prefabrication of American shopping malls, etc.

(3.13) Pronunciation – elision

Aim

To help students understand when elision takes place and practise using it.

Procedure

Write **bus stop** on the board and ask students to pronounce it without a break between the two words and slightly elongating the /s/ sound. Then rub out the two s's and replace them with one large one joining the two words, like this:

bu ʃ top

Do the same with **big car**. This will help your students 'see' what happens when elision takes place. You should also point out in this second example that the elided sounds are not exactly the same. A short 'glottal stop' (a sound like a quick cough or 'catch' in the throat) appears between the words: / bɪʔkɑː /.

Now ask students to practise the examples in the Student's Book in pairs. When they have finished, play the tape, stopping after each example to allow round the class repetition.

Key

1 junctio*n*ine
2 har*t*imes
3 fre*sh*rimps
4 fin*t*ime
5 fu*l*ength
6 dee*b*lue
7 hal*f*ull
8 gin an*t*onic
9 dar*g*reen
10 ho*d*ish

Tapescript

1 junction nine
2 hard times
3 fresh shrimps
4 find time
5 full length
6 deep blue
7 half full
8 gin and tonic
9 dark green
10 hot dish

(3.14) Review

Aim

To review selected language items from Unit 2.

Procedure

Ask students to do the task individually and then compare answers in pairs. If they have doubts, allow them to refer back to the previous unit. Check answers through open-class feedback.

Key

1 colour   2 leading   3 stressed   4 heredity
5 heartbeat   6 cholesterol   7 vigorous
8 unwelcome   9 bay   10 beans

Crime never pays?

4.1 To start you thinking

Aim

To introduce students to the theme of the unit and encourage a personalised response.

Procedure

a Give students a few minutes to read through the questions and think of their answers.

b Put students in groups of three or four and give them a time limit of five to ten minutes. Then get some open-class feedback on who in each group has had the strangest/worst/luckiest/etc. experience. You may also like to tell the class about anything that has happened to you.

4.2 Reading

Aim

To practise scanning.
To provide a lead-in to the discussion.

Procedure

Make sure the students read the questions before they read the text.

Key

(suggested answers)

1 They thought a crime involved the whole community, not just the victim.
2 It meant it was a very serious crime.
3 All adult males in the community.
4 Men responsible for keeping the peace.
5 The Saxon name for a law court.
6 He had to raise a hue and cry so other men could help him catch the criminal.
7 It comes from *shire reeve*, meaning the judge in more serious cases in a shire.
8 A group of men that a sheriff could call up to help him catch a criminal.

4.3 Discussion

Aim

To personalise the unit topic further and encourage fluency.

Procedure

Put students in groups of four and set a time limit of ten minutes. Tell each group to appoint a secretary to note down the group's findings and decisions. At the end of the discussions, each group must report back its conclusions to the whole class.

Key

3 Neighbourhood Watch consists of neighbours in the same street grouping together to keep an eye on each other's properties, especially when they are away on holiday, and informing the police of anything suspicious they see happening in the street.

4.4 Collocations

Aim

To extend students' knowledge of collocations related to the unit theme.

Procedure

Ask students to do the task individually and then check answers in pairs.

Key

2 i 3 k 4 j 5 a 6 c 7 d 8 l 9 b 10 f
11 h 12 g

(4.5) Reading

Aim

To improve the students' understanding of links between sentences.

Procedure

Ask the students to read through the eight sentences, and then, working individually or in pairs, put them in order.

It is important, when you feed back, to spend time discussing why one order is better than another. This discussion will help the students to focus on various ways in which sentences are linked together in English. At this stage, be positive towards any suggestions that are well-justified even if they are not the 'correct' ones.

> ### Key
>
> B, E, C, A, F, H, G, D
> (Also possible is B, E, C, A, G, F, H, D)

(4.6) Writing – achieving formal style

Aim

To revise and extend the idea of formal style.

Procedure

Remind students of the formal letter layout they looked at in 3.9. Then go through the six points of formal style in the Student's Book, at each point asking students to supply further examples if possible.

Then give students five minutes to read through Jack Brown's letter individually. In pairs, they should then go through it again in more detail, analysing how the style can be improved.

When they have finished, go through a good version orally, with students chipping in their ideas.

> ### Key
>
> (suggested answer – see letter following)

57 Bath Rd
Barford BF8 3DX

Dear Mr Payne,

I am writing to express my concern about the alarming numbers of juvenile delinquents in my neighbourhood. The area is in an appalling state, with abandoned and vandalised cars littering the streets and walls covered in graffiti. It really is most unsightly. The area has become so dangerous that recently my nextdoor neighbour was attacked and robbed in broad daylight. Needless to say, she was deeply shocked and distressed by the incident.

The reason for this escalation of crime would seem to lie as much with the police as with the young offenders. There are very few police patrols in the area and when an incident does occur, the police appear ineffectual. Indeed, they seem to do little more than make some brief enquiries before returning to the police station, presumably, to file yet another report.

I feel, therefore, that I must insist steps are taken to address this problem of policing. Moreover, I must urge you to look into the question of custodial sentences for young offenders, as it seems abundantly clear that cautions and probationary sentences achieve very little.

I look forward to hearing from you.

Yours sincerely

Jack Brown

Jack Brown

(4.7) Reading

Aim

To practise vocabulary (especially collocations) to do with crime and the police.

Procedure

Ask the students to find out the meanings of the words in the box before they start to read the passage.

This can be done either by pre-teaching them yourself, or by asking students, in pairs, to find out the meanings from a good dictionary (preferably monolingual).

Then, individually, the students read through the passage to get the general meaning without, at this stage, writing in any words. They should then (in pairs) write in the easier words, which will give them more information on which to base their attempts for the others.

Key

2 officers   3 burglaries   4 sniffer
5 warrant   6 custody   7 bail   8 cautioned
9 charge   10 raid   11 observations
12 patrols   13 recover   14 partnership

4.8 Vocabulary

Aim

To review and extend topic vocabulary and encourage students to use a technique for recording 'loose' collocations.

Procedure

a Explain to your students how a keyword grid works, i.e. that you record useful vocabulary around a keyword

e.g. She never broke the law but occasionally bent it!

Also explain that keyword grids grow over time. In other words, there are more words that collocate loosely with *law* and so students should draw their own keyword grids in their notebooks and then add to them as they meet more possible collocations.

Now ask your students to make short sentences with *law* and its loose collocations to check they have understood the concept. Point out that they will have to add articles where necessary and that this is true of all keyword grids.

b Ask students to do the task individually and then check answers in pairs or small groups.

c Ask students to do the task individually and then check answers in pairs.

Key

b

Verbs	Describing words	Keyword	Words that come after
commit carry out investigate	serious petty perfect	the/a CRIME	of passion buster wave writer
arrest track down convict punish sentence… to	dangerous hardened	the /a CRIMINAL	court damage investigation record mind
call join inform cooperate with	uniformed undercover plain-clothes	the /a POLICE	station force custody officer dog car presence man/woman headquarters

c   1 crime of passion   2 petty crime   3 join … force   4 Undercover police
5 police custody   6 crime writer   7 crime wave   8 criminal record
9 police presence   10 hardened criminal

**EXTRA COMMUNICATION ACTIVITY
MAY BE DONE HERE** *(see page 117)*

4.9 # Grammar – reported speech

Aim

This section looks at the relationship between direct and reported speech, which the students should have studied before, and reviews and consolidates the rules involved in transforming one into the other.

Anticipated problems

- Although most of the details are not too difficult, there are quite a few of them. Encourage students to remember that there are six main rules, which they should be able to recall at will.

- The use of back spacing, i.e. moving tenses into the past in reported speech, is an area of English which is changing. The modern trend is not to back space for things that are still true, but this is not consistently used.

- Back spacing into the Past Perfect is not always used, but students are best advised to apply the rule for safety.

Procedure

a Allow students a few moments to study the text in boxes 1–4. Ask them what the sentences in boxes 1 and 3 have in common and elicit that they are reported speech. Ask students to complete the sentence in box 4, check their answers and correct any mistakes, but don't spend time explaining corrections at this stage. Tell them they are going to look at the rules in a minute.

b Ask students to do this in pairs.

Before you check their answers, tell them to look at the rules again, and go through them dealing with any problems. You may need to give more examples on the board.

Ask them to look at their answers again and make any necessary corrections.

Check the answers as a whole class.

c Ask students to do this on their own, then to check it with their partners.

Check the answers as a whole class.

Ask the students to find more examples of the rules in the other sentences.

d Ask students to do this in pairs. Monitor closely, directing them back to the relevant rules where necessary.

Check the answers as a whole class.

Key

a *it isn't worth putting*

b Answers may vary but should contain the following information:

2 The police claimed that figures published earlier <u>that day</u> showed a big drop in crime in the <u>previous</u> month.

3 The judge told <u>him</u> that if <u>she</u> heard about <u>him</u> battering <u>his</u> wife again, <u>he</u> could expect a prison sentence.

4 He said he'<u>ll</u> pick us up about two.

5 The social worker <u>warned</u> him of the dangers of mixing with other ex-prisoners.

6 Judy asked where <u>I'd bought</u> the handcuffs and how much <u>they'd cost</u>.

c 2 Figures published earlier today show a big drop in crime last month.

3 If I hear about you battering your wife again, you can expect a prison sentence.

4 I'll pick you up about two.

5 Answers will vary, e.g. It's dangerous for you to mix with other ex-prisoners because it might lead you back into a life of crime.

6 Where did you buy the handcuffs and how much did they cost?

d 1 The shopkeeper said/stated that the man had been wearing a blue T-shirt. (*was wearing* is possible)

2 Mrs Jackson at number 27 said it was/had been the same man she had seen the day before when she had gone/been to the hairdresser's.

3 A passer-by said/claimed that the police never patrolled around there/in that district any more.

4 The bank manager refused to tell us anything./The bank manager said he/she wasn't going to tell us anything.

(4.10) Listening

Aim

To understand the main events in a long and convoluted story.

Procedure

Pre-teach *ram-raiding* by referring students to the picture in the Student's Book, and asking them what is happening.

a

> **(F)** **Suggested Focus Task:**
>
> Put the students in small groups and ask them to try to predict the main points of the story, using the eight statements in the Student's Book. Stress that this will help them to be better listeners, and it does not matter if they are right or not.

Explain that they are going to listen to a longish story, and that it is not necessary to understand every word.

Play the tape **once only**. There is sufficient redundancy in the story for them to be able to do the task with just one listening. (Only if they are really struggling should you play it a second time.)

Then ask students to compare their answers in pairs and small groups, and then feed back to the whole class.

b Use the same procedure again.

> **Key**
>
> **a** Correct order: 3, 5, 2, 1, 7, 8, 4, 6
> **b** 1 False 2 True 3 False 4 False 5 True

Tapescript

VOICE 1: And on this particular occasion, which was quite late in December, um … my colleague, Matt, and I were out in a car and we were sent to a ram-raid in progress, which obviously means it's happening at the time. Anyway, we came round the corner and, sure enough, embedded in this shop front is a car and outside the shop facing towards us is another car, quite a big estate car with its lights on. And, as we pulled up, the estate car pulled off towards us and was coming pretty much head-on. And I was driving, managed to swerve to one side and it just sort of caught the wing of our car and carried on going up on the pavement and passed us. And then out of the shop came two other people and they were wearing balaclavas and red Santa hats with bobbles, and they ran out and we stopped our car and then we both grabbed a person each and we were both wrestling with our prisoners, trying to gain control of them. Matt suddenly started screaming and I looked up to see the estate car that had pulled away was blocking my view of him and I could only hear him screaming and um … I shouted to him, what's the matter? And he said 'Just stay with him', meaning the person I was with and so I did but it was quite a dilemma as to whether or not to go and help him and leave my prisoner. And so in the end I decided to stay with my prisoner because I thought well, if Matt isn't seriously injured then at least I'll have caught a prisoner and if he is seriously injured, I'll want to get at least one of the people that is sort of responsible for it. So anyway eventually this estate drove away and I carried on concentrating on my prisoner and then Matt shouts, 'Get out of the road!' and I looked up to see the estate car reversing at speed towards me. And I was on my knees with my prisoner and if it had hit me, it would have been head-high, and it would have been pretty nasty but fortunately I managed to dive out of the road and drag my prisoner with me into a doorway, still scrapping. And I remember just looking up at the estate car which was sort of hovering beside me, thinking any second now these people in the car are going to come out and they're going to rescue their fourth man and at that moment another police car came round the corner and the estate drove off and I just waved at the police car to go after that car. Matt had had to let go of his prisoner and I managed to keep mine and some other officers came along and helped. Anyway, it turned out that Matt had been lying on the pavement, wrestling, and his legs were in the road and the car had come along and driven over his ankles backwards and forwards in an attempt to free their friend and fortunately he had some big boots on and um … he managed to get away with just bruises, which was quite amazing cos there's some pretty impressive tyre marks over his boots, which he's kept for posterity. And the car that was being chased, the estate car, which by this time had three people in it, with Matt's prisoner, had something wrong with it, so they had to abandon it a few yards down the road. And two of them ran off and were quickly caught and one ran up on to the rooftops and was chased by a dog handler and his dog, amazingly, on the rooftops but then they went down a very big drop to a very low rooftop and he'd have injured the dog if he'd let the dog go down there; so the officer put a special harness on to the dog and lowered it down on to the lower roof and um … and then jumped down himself and they managed to get the fourth man. And so they were all arrested and they all went to court and they all got three years in prison.

VOICE 2: And you got an award. Is that right?

VOICE 1: Yeah, Matt and I got a commendation for bravery because we'd sort of been ruthless and held on to our prisoners despite being injured.

(4.11) Pronunciation – sentence stress

Aim

To help students understand why some words are stressed and others unstressed in native speaker speech and to give them practice in reproducing this.

Procedure

a The input for this activity is on the tape. Play the introductory part and make sure students follow in their books. Get them to practise with the tape but don't expect perfection – approximation is the goal!

b First play the tape sentence by sentence, allowing time for the students to mark the stressed and unstressed words with bubbles. Then rewind and let students practise saying the sentences with the tape. This can be done individually around the class as well as with the whole group chorusing.

Key and tapescript

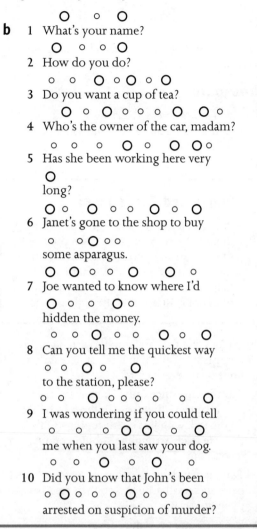

b
1 What's your name?
2 How do you do?
3 Do you want a cup of tea?
4 Who's the owner of the car, madam?
5 Has she been working here very long?
6 Janet's gone to the shop to buy some asparagus.
7 Joe wanted to know where I'd hidden the money.
8 Can you tell me the quickest way to the station, please?
9 I was wondering if you could tell me when you last saw your dog.
10 Did you know that John's been arrested on suspicion of murder?

(4.12) Review

Aim

To review selected language items from Unit 3.

Procedure

Ask students to do the task individually and then compare answers in pairs. If they have doubts, allow them to refer back to the previous unit. Check answers through open-class feedback.

Key

1 sandy beaches   2 spectacular scenery
3 crystal clear water   4 tourist trap
5 day-trippers   6 scenic route
7 long-haul plane journey   8 insect bites

You are what you eat

5.1 To start you thinking

Aim

To introduce students to the theme of the unit through personalisation.

Procedure

a Ask students to do the task individually and to spend no more than two or three minutes on it.

b Use this activity to create a check-list on the board of healthy and unhealthy foods. Many of these will be personal opinions and should provide a point for discussion.

5.2 Reading

Aim

To predict the vocabulary in a passage.
To prepare the students for the language work in 5.5.

Procedure

a Ask students to justify their answers to these two questions. If you think the discussion might be leading on to sensitive areas, cut it short.

b The students should do this activity in pairs or small groups if possible.

Key

a They live in the Greek countryside.

b The following are mentioned: cereals, salad, olive oil, beans, lentils, vegetables, fruit, milk, cheese, fish, wine.

5.3 Grammar – relative pronouns

Aim

This is an opportunity to check students' detailed understanding of relative clauses. 5.3 looks at the uses of relative pronouns and the relative adverb *where*.

Anticipated problems

Even at advanced levels, students' knowledge of this area is often still patchy. Typical problems include:

- the false idea that *whose* cannot refer to things and places, as in:
  - *Health foods, whose high prices had become notorious, were finally taken seriously by supermarkets.*
  - *An area whose climate is hotter tends to use a larger variety of ingredients in its dishes.*
- the false idea that *where* is the only relative word used for places. This leads to errors of over-use like:
  - **He owns a little place where serves the best pasta in town.*

The problem here is that a pronoun is needed (*which*) but *where* is a relative adverb; it cannot be used as the subject or object of a relative clause:

- *That's the hospital where/in which I study nutrition.*
- *That's the hospital which (not where) teaches nutrition.*

Generally speaking, *where* has the meaning of *which* + preposition.

Procedure

You could begin with a game to tune students' minds to the target language.

Put them into two groups and give each group a word to define using *which* or *who*. This is a chance to recycle earlier vocabulary, e.g.

A sniffer dog (Unit 4) *... is a dog which ...*

a Ask students to work individually before checking the answers as a class. You could inform them that there are five more items to find, but this should be unnecessary at this level.

Ask which word is the adverb (*where*; it doesn't act as a noun – see above).

b Ask students to work in pairs, giving each other examples of how the words can be used if they disagree.

Check the answers as a whole class.

c Ask students to work individually, then to compare their answers with a partner.

Check the answers as a whole class and answer any queries on form or meaning.

Key

a A fanatical vegetarian **whom** I know was telling me about the virtues of the Greek diet. Greek villagers, **whose** lifestyle can be quite harsh, are said to live to a ripe old age despite a relative lack of health care. And the reason? Research suggests it's the food they eat **that** keeps them in good health. Their staple foods, **which** consist mainly of fresh fruit and vegetables, are known to be beneficial to anyone **who** eats them in sufficient quantities. What a surprising unforeseen advantage of living in a country **where** meat is expensive – still, I don't think I'll be giving up the finer foods in life just yet!

b

Pronoun /adverb	Person	Thing	Place	Formal only
whom	✓	✗	✗	✓
whose	✓	✓	✓	✗
that	✓	✓	✓	✗
which	✗	✓	✓	✗
who	✓	✗	✗	✗
where	✗	✗	✓	✗

c 2 who 3 which 4 that/which/✗
5 which/whom 6 who 7 which
8 whose

5.4

Grammar – relative causes

Aim

5.4 focuses on the differences between defining and non-defining relative clauses in terms of:

● form, i.e. appropriate use of *which* versus *that*, and the importance of commas.

● meaning, i.e. a defining clause specifies what is being referred to in the main clause whereas a non-defining clause merely adds supplementary information.

● register or degree of formality.

Anticipated problems

Typical problems include:

● the lack of awareness that a comma can make so much difference to the actual meaning, rather than being simply a detail of style.

● difficulties with the use of *which* in non-defining clauses, where it can refer back not only to a specific noun, but also to the overall meaning of the entire preceding clause, as in:

– *I love apples, which are so healthy.*

– *I love apples, which is lucky because we have lots of apple trees in our garden.*

Procedure

a To introduce the concept and terms, put the following sentences on the board:

1 *The students who loved their teacher bought her a present.*

2 *The students, who loved their teacher, bought her a present.*

Ask what the difference is and give students a few minutes to talk about it with a partner. Then ask them to explain. You need to explain if they can't. (In 1, the relative clause is defining. Not everyone bought the present and it specifies who did. In 2, everyone bought the present and the non-defining clause, as extra information, tells us they also loved their teacher.)

Ask students to work together in pairs.

Monitor closely pointing out the relevant information and giving clues where necessary.

Check the answers as a whole class and answer any queries on form or meaning.

b Ask students to work individually.

Ask students to compare their answers in pairs, explaining the reasons for their choices.

Check the answers as a whole class.

Key

a 1 a) is non-defining; all the meat had been stored in the ship's fridge, and it was all unsafe – the clause merely gives more information about it. In b), only the meat in the ship's fridge was unsafe, and presumably there was other meat which was not – the clause defines the meat that was unsafe. In b), *which* can be replaced by *that*, but not in a).

2 a) is natural, neutral English; you could use it in any situation except the most formal – b) is highly formal and/or old-fashioned.

Key (cont)

3 In **a)**, *which* refers to cooking meals on an old fire, i.e. the whole of the previous clause. In **b)**, *which* refers only to the gas fire itself.

4 There is very little difference – **a)** is typical conversational English – **b)** is slightly more formal, or just more careful.

5 *Whom* is the relative pronoun used when the person is the object of the relative clause, but its use nowadays is regarded as highly formal – *who* is much more common (though still disapproved of by some people, as is ending a sentence with a preposition). *Whom* is obligatory if you bring the preposition to the front of the clause, a formal construction more common in written English.

b 1 *Chefs **who** own restaurants have much more control over what is on the menu.*

This must be defining because not all chefs own restaurants and this sentence is saying that if they do own the restaurant, they have more control.
There should be no commas.

2 *I brought some excellent wines back from Bordeaux, **which** is the first French city I've visited.*

This must be non-defining – there is only one Bordeaux in France and so information about my visit cannot define it; it is merely extra information. There must be a comma before *which*.

3 *I hate peanuts, **which** is the reason I'm not fond of many Thai dishes.*

This must be non-defining. The clause simply gives a result of my dislike of peanuts and in no way defines any particular peanuts – it needs a comma before *which*.

4 *I respect anyone **whose** knowledge of wines is as great as my own – though there aren't many around of course!*

This must be defining – the speaker is specifying the limited number of people s/he respects. There should be no commas.

5 *People **who** smoke tend to have a much weaker sense of taste.*

This must be defining – there is a particular group of people, i.e. smokers, who have a weakened sense of taste.

6 *Simon Talbot, **whose** sea-food restaurant has five stars in Gourmet's Guide, is advertising a training course for new chefs.*

This is non-defining – it is not distinguishing between more than one Simon Talbot, rather providing extra information about him. There should be commas before and after the relative clause.

7 *The British beef industry, **which** had major exports in the early 1990s, suffered badly from the effects of Mad Cow Disease before it was brought under control.*

This is non-defining – it is talking about the beef industry as a whole, and the information on exports is supplementary. There should be commas before and after the relative clause.

(Students may think that it could be defining by referring only to that part of the beef industry that suffered, thus suggesting there were other parts that didn't. However, if this were the intended meaning, a word like *part* would be used in the sentence.)

8 *The English food at the barbecue was really boring, but I loved the food **which/that** was from the Caribbean.*

This must be defining to tell us which particular food was loved – it cannot have a comma before *which/that*.

9 *The factory **where** my friend works makes most of the frozen food you see in supermarkets.*

This must be defining to tell us which factory – it cannot have a comma before *where*.

10 *I've never eaten anything in my life **which/that** has made me so ill.*

This is defining and tells us that the person ate something which gave him/her the worst food poisoning they have ever had. There should be no comma before *which/that*. (Students may think that it could be non-defining, but this would mean that the person has never eaten anything, and that is the reason s/he is ill, which is obviously nonsense!)

5.5 To start you thinking

Aim

To extend students' vocabulary and prepare them for the following reading passage.

Procedure

Students should attempt to complete the task individually first and then compare and discuss answers in pairs.

> ### Key
>
> 1 shark 2 whale 3 clam 4 cod 5 crab
> 6 octopus 7 eel 8 prawn

5.6 Reading

Aim

To give the students the opportunity to read an extended text.
To practise interpreting a text from textual clues.
To guess the meaning of vocabulary items from the context.

Procedure

a This is a scanning exercise, to orientate the students within the text, which is from *Moby-Dick* by Herman Melville. If you feel a literary text is not useful for your students, then omit this part. However, the skills practised can apply to any text. Do not let the students spend more than a couple of minutes on the text – tell them they will have a chance to read it in more detail later.

b Give the students plenty of time to read the passage in detail. This exercise deals with points of interpretation and speculation, which are different from the kinds of exercises so far in this book, and require a fairly detailed and reflective reading of the text.

The amount of time you wish to spend on this section will depend on the interests and needs of your students, although the techniques required would be useful for any kind of text. Allow plenty of time for discussion and argument, and in particular, get students to justify their answers by reference to the text.

c As always with this kind of activity, the important part is the students' explanation of how they came to their choices. Make sure that there is ample time for this.

> ### Key
>
> **a** 1 shark, whale, clam, cod
>   2 a kind of soup
>
> **b** (suggested answers)
>
> 1 A novel. This is suggested by the use of the past tense to narrate the story, the use of dialogue, the literary style (*Upon making known …*).
>
> 2 No. They use a lamp to light their way upstairs; the account books are covered in shark-skin; a great deal of the vocabulary is old-fashioned (*to attend to all his affairs, I assure ye, we despatched it with great expedition*); also the setting which involves boats and fishermen.
>
> 3 Subjective response, but probably: ironic, amusing, poetic(?).
>
> 4 Subjective response, but they are travelling by boat (see line 2), and seem to be on a long voyage, since they are staying in hotels along the way. Queequeg is a whaleman (line 71) with a harpoon, so perhaps they are looking for, and presumably hunting, whales.
>
> 5 Subjective response.
>
> 6 They are both men (line 80) so perhaps colleagues or companions? The writer seems to be superior in some way (he answers for Queequeg in line 70, and is the one to go to the kitchen in line 42), so perhaps master and servant? Or, as they are sailing, perhaps captain and mate?
>
> 7 Whalemen.
>
> 8 No. In the first paragraph, it says they had been recommended there by the landlord of another inn.
>
> 9 abrupt (she just says '*Clam or cod?*' with no polite forms)
>   loud (she *bawls*)
>   strict (she won't let Queequeg take his harpoon to the room)
>
> 10 The writer believes Mrs Hussey is offering them a single clam (rather than clam soup), which he does not think will be enough.
>
> 11 The chowders; the clam-shells in the paving; Mrs Hussey's necklace; the shark-skin on the account books; the flavour of the milk; the cow with its feet in the cod's head.
>
> 12 Because a previous guest had been found dead with a harpoon in his side.
>
> 13 The harpoon.
>
> **c** 1 clam 2 hearken 3 chowder 4 repast
>   5 snugly 6 ashore 7 bawl 8 usher

Vocabulary

Aim

To review and extend topic vocabulary and encourage students to use a vocabulary recording technique already presented in the book.

Procedure

a Ask students to do the task individually and then check answers in pairs.

b Ask students to do the task individually and then check answers in pairs.

> ### Key
>
> **a** clam, cod, chowder, hazel nuts, biscuit, salted pork, butter, pepper, salt, eel, shark, milk, smoked herring.
>
> **b** Words from the passage could include: clam (under *sea-food*); smoked herring, eel, shark (under *fish*); salted pork (under *types of meat*); milk (under either *food* or *dairy products*). Other combinations are possible.

5.8 ## Idioms from food and eating

Aim

To practise the skill of guessing vocabulary from context.
To extend students' knowledge of idioms connected with food and drink and fix them in students' minds through contrast with their mother tongue.

Procedure

a Ask the students to read through the idioms and think what they might mean. Then put them in pairs and ask them to compare ideas. With the students still in pairs or small groups, play the dialogues twice (at least) and ask them to work out the approximate meanings of the idioms from context. Stop after each dialogue to give them the chance to reflect. Stress that they do not need to understand every word of the dialogues to be able to do this.

b Put students in groups of three or four for this task. If you have a multilingual class, mix up the nationalities as much as possible. Students must give a word for word translation of the idioms for this task to be memorable!

> ### Key
>
> **a** 1 (I wouldn't do it) under any circumstances
> 2 crushed together, with little or no space between them
> 3 completely mad
> 4 to eat too much
> 5 a very important person in an organisation
> 6 a very good thing indeed, new and exciting
> 7 no (journalist) who is good at their job
> 8 in (or near) poverty
> 9 to get someone out of a difficult or dangerous situation
> 10 something to think about carefully

Tapescript

1 **MAN 1:** Do you fancy going parachuting some time?
   MAN 2: Parachuting? *Parachuting?* You must be joking! I wouldn't go parachuting for all the tea in China …
   MAN 1: Afraid, are we?
   MAN 2: You bet I am! What happens if the thing doesn't open?

2 **WOMAN:** Good journey home, dear?
   MAN: Since you ask, no. The train was 45 minutes late, and then we were packed like sardines into the carriage.
   WOMAN: Lucky you had a shower this morning, then.
   MAN: Unfortunately, that wasn't true of the people crushed up against me …

3 **WOMAN:** Of course, he's a lovely man, but as nutty as a fruitcake.
   MAN: Really? You mean he's a bit on the odd side?
   WOMAN: Well, more than odd, I'd say. He keeps his slippers in the fridge. Says he likes to keep his feet cool.
   MAN: That's not so much eccentric as completely loony.
   WOMAN: Well, there you go.

4 **WOMAN:** How was last night?
   MAN: All right. John made a pig of himself, as usual.
   WOMAN: Did he? Perhaps he hadn't had anything to eat at lunchtime.
   MAN: Oh yes he had! He went out with Marie-Claude at lunchtime to that new brasserie in Lamb Street.

5 **WOMAN:** Did you know that Frank's become a really big cheese in the EU?

MAN: Frank? What, Frank Parsons? That little squit in the Research Department?

WOMAN: Yes, he's become something like Deputy Head of the Department of Statistics, or Information.

MAN: Does he have to live in Brussels, then?

WOMAN: Mmm, well, he has a flat there, and comes back home at weekends.

6 MAN 1: Have you seen this new programme on Channel 4? The one with the two men who live on a boat.

MAN 2: 'Men Boating Badly', you mean? Oh God yes, and I've bought all the videos as well.

MAN 1: Oh, you haven't! It's not that good!

MAN 2: It is! As far as I'm concerned, it's the best thing since sliced bread.

7 WOMAN 1: Liz has got a new job on the Newcastle Evening Post.

WOMAN 2: What, you mean she's moving from London?

WOMAN 1: Yup! from March.

WOMAN 2: A bad move, I'd say. No journalist worth their salt would work outside London.

WOMAN 1: I disagree! There's plenty going on in Newcastle.

WOMAN 2: That's not the point. London is where the *important* things happen …

8 MAN 1: And you can see all around you that the standard of living is getting better all the time.

MAN 2: Absolute poppycock. The number of people living on the breadline has increased significantly since the present government came to power.

MAN 1: I'm sorry, but there is no evidence whatsoever for that assertion …

9 MAN 1: What happened, then, on Tuesday? Did you get in all right?

MAN 2: Oh God, don't talk about it. I was nearly an hour late. But luckily the boss had a meeting that morning, so she never saw me come in. And then later Carol really saved my bacon by telling her I came in on time that day.

MAN 1: Blimey! That was good of her. Why'd she do that, then?

MAN 2: Dunno. Must fancy me.

10 WOMAN 1: Don't you think this means the end of the whole operation? Now that Brookes has gone, we'll have to change everything.

WOMAN 2: No, I don't think that, actually. But his decision to resign has certainly given us food for thought.

WOMAN 1: Food for thought! Is that all you can say? We've got to *do* something!

EXTRA COMMUNICATION ACTIVITY MAY BE DONE HERE *(see page 118)*

5.9 Hearing perception

Aim and procedure

See Introduction.

Tapescript

(*=tone)

And it's one of those restaurants *that you see all over France *where basically they offer a menu for that day *which means you have no choice about what you eat *you just turn up and buy the menu *this was a fifty franc menu *and the first thing that happened when you walk into the restaurant and sit down is that they just *well … paper cloth on the table and they put *a large bottle of red wine and a large basket of bread *on the table in front of you. *Now that is a delightful way to start any meal. *For me it was almost enough! *It was then followed by a fantastic home made vegetable soup *gallons of it and every time we finished the bowl *it was refilled, because they obviously thought we wanted more *although we were desperately trying to finish it not to be rude and leave some *we didn't realise the etiquette of the situation.

5.10 Pronunciation – contrastive stress

Aim

To highlight the importance of stress as a way of contrasting with or correcting what has been stated previously and to give students practice in this.

Procedure

Write the number 56 on the board and elicit how this would normally be pronounced and where the stress would normally go

○ ○ **O**

i.e. fifty six.

Now write up the following dialogue:

A: How old is he?

B: 56, I think.

A: Sorry, did you say 56 or 66?

and elicit from your students how the third line would be pronounced:

○ ○ ○   ○ ○ ○

Sorry, did you say fifty six or sixty six?

and why (because the stress contrasts the two areas of meaning which are in doubt). Make sure students can say this sentence with the correct stress pattern before proceeding.

a Students do this task individually and then compare answers in pairs or small groups. If your students' stress is generally poor, ask them to repeat the sentences after the tape. Check answers through open-class feedback.

b Ask students to predict where the stress will go before playing the tape. Students do this task individually and then compare answers in pairs or small groups. Check answers through open-class feedback.

c Practise with the whole class first. Use stronger students to help the weaker ones, rather than simply supplying the correct version yourself (or by using the tape). Go round the class and monitor performance.

d Put students in pairs for this light-hearted practice on corrective stress. Spend a little time setting up the situation and giving examples of the task by asking a strong or confident student to play the part of the chef with you as the personal assistant. Give the students plenty of time to think before they start speaking. During the pair work, go round and monitor performance. At the end, ask the best pairs to act the scene out in front of the class.

Key and tapescript

a 1   ○
He used to live in London.

    2 ○
fish pie   3 ○
go on a diet

    4 ○ ○
two hundred and forty-five milligrams

    5 ○ ○
it was made from beef and potatoes

    6 ○ ○
you have to boil it for about ten minutes

    7 ○ ○ ○
six seven double two nine four

    8 ○ ○
John MacDonald

b 1 He's worked in London, hasn't he?

       ○
No, he used to live in London, but he's never worked there.

    2 You're going to have the cottage pie, then?

       ○
No, I'm going to have the fish pie. John's having the cottage pie.

---

3 I'm surprised Fiona's given up her diet.

       ○
No, I said she's decided to go on a diet.

4 Peter said the result was three hundred and forty-five milligrams.

    ○
Two hundred and forty-five milligrams, you mean …

5 And it's made from beef and potatoes, is it?

    ○
No, it was made from beef and potatoes, but that was before the beef scare!

6 So you fry it for ten minutes …

    ○
No, you have to boil it for about ten minutes.

7 Is your fax number six four double two nine four?

    ○
Six seven double two nine four.

8 Did you say John O'Donald?

    ○
John MacDonald.

(5.11) **Review**

Aim

To review selected language items from Unit 4.

Procedure

Ask students to do the task individually and then compare answers in pairs. If they have doubts, allow them to refer back to the previous unit. Check answers through open-class feedback.

Key

2 custody 3 bail 4 evidence 5 red-handed
6 property 7 raid 8 refused

Money makes the world go round

6.1 To start you thinking

Aim

To introduce students to the theme of the unit by discussing common sayings.

Procedure

Start by explaining any potentially problematic language items e.g. 'Neither a … nor a … be' (archaic) means 'Don't be a … or a … '. Then put students into pairs or small groups to discuss the meaning of each saying and whether it shows money to be a good thing, a bad thing or neither. After five to ten minutes, get some open-class feedback on what the pairs/groups have decided.

Key

1 People with money can use it to persuade others to do what they want. 2 The desire for money is the basis of crime and corruption. 3 If a stupid person has a lot of money, s/he will soon lose it to other more intelligent people. 4 Everyone is corruptible through money or some other inducement. 5 A way of making money without having to do anything hard. 6 If you are careful with money, you soon amass savings. 7 You can avoid a lot of problems by neither borrowing nor lending money and other things. 8 Love cannot be bought no matter how much money you have. 9 People with money appear to have a good time while people without appear to suffer. 10 Money is valuable and should not be wasted.

Money as a good thing: 6
Money as a bad thing: 1, 2, 4, 7, 8, 9
Money as a neutral thing: 3, 5, 10

6.2 Reading

Aim

To understand the main points in a passage.
To understand implied meaning in a passage.

Procedure

a Start by asking students whether there is a National Lottery in their own countries. Do they ever play? Have they ever won? Do they know anyone who has? Who benefits from the lottery? etc.

Ask students to read the statements before they read the text. This reading should be swift, and can be done individually or in pairs. When you feed back to the whole class, make sure the students justify their answers by referring back to the text.

b In this part, students consider the writer's implication or indirect meaning.

Ask the students to read the text again, more carefully this time, and, individually, answer the questions. Then they should compare answers in pairs or small groups. Once again, ask for justifications when feeding back.

Key

a 1 Cross 2 Cross 3 Cross (39 states)
4 Tick (4.48x20=89.6)
5 Cross (no statistics on this) 6 Tick

b 1 Camelot is the (private) company that runs the National Lottery in Britain (and makes huge profits). 2 He means money. 3 It's based on the saying *It's the rich that get the pleasure. It's the poor that get the blame.* 4 Because he thinks it isn't a good cause. 5 Rather negative – he thinks his wife will be happy to be divorced from him! 6 The implications are that money 'drops from heaven'. 7 Punter means person who buys a ticket (in this case).

8 Because occasionally a poor person wins and becomes rich but generally poor people spend a lot of money on the lottery for no benefit at all.

6.3 Discussion

Aim

To prepare students for the following reading section and encourage fluency.

Procedure

Put students in groups of three or four. Start things off (if you consider it suitable) by admitting something you have done for money but now regret. Monitor discussions and conclude before the groups start running out of steam. Get a little open-class feedback before moving on.

6.4 Reading

Aim

To predict the contents of a passage from the title. To interpret the basic meaning of a passage from a gap-filling exercise.

Procedure

a and **b**

Start by writing the title of the passage on the board. Ask the students to work in pairs and small groups. Encourage students to use some of the vocabulary that might have come up in 6.3.

It is not so important that students get the right words but rather that they start thinking in the right area. Students can check individually or in the same pairs.

c This is not a test. Rather, it should encourage students to see the way a text might develop its meaning over the course of several paragraphs. For that reason, encourage the students to look at the text before and after each space.

When you feed back, make sure the students justify their answers.

Key

c A1, B6, C3, D2, E5

6.5 Discourse

Aim

To work on reference within a text.

Procedure

Make sure the students are familiar with the idea of reference within a text, and in particular that a word like it can refer to different words in the same or a different sentence, depending on context and meaning. If they have problems with this, do the first one with the whole class.

Key

1 The idea that you can break the law if large sums of money are involved but you can't break the law over a few pounds.
2 many people in society 3 world
4 one famous banker 5 father's brother
6 my mother and father's 7 (bank) notes
8 (mother's) family 9 hole punch
10 stealing small items (stationery in this case) from the company one works for

6.6 Writing – giving examples

Aim

To encourage students to include examples in their written work.

Procedure

Start by writing the following sentence on the board:

There are many everyday objects which were unheard of even twenty years ago.

Ask how this sentence might be improved. Elicit the use of examples to make the content more interesting. Then draw the students' attention to the two ways of connecting examples to the remainder of the text which are outlined in the Student's Book.

Then go through the expressions in the box, taking care to point out the formality of the expressions *examples abound*, *examples include* and *exemplified by ...*

Key

(suggested answers only; accept any other correct versions)

1 … including rampant inflation and devaluation.

2 … Take for instance the once-great football star George Best.

3 … such as a company car or subsidised meals.

4 … Credit and debit cards spring to mind.

5 … from lottery scratch cards to betting on the horses.

6 … One obvious example is through the Co-operative Bank.

7 … like books, shoes, clothes and suchlike.

8 … Examples include the famous 'window tax' of the 18th century.

9 … from rude cashiers to wrongly calculated interest repayments.

10 … checking your change in shops and your bank statement for mistakes, to name but a few.

11 … e.g. the US dollar, the Deutschmark or the Japanese yen.

12 … for example personal pension plans, share investment, etc.

EXTRA COMMUNICATION ACTIVITY MAY BE DONE HERE *(see page 119)*

6.7 Grammar – ~*ing* forms

Aim

The range of ways ~ing forms operate in English is very broad with some quite dissimilar applications. The aim here is to raise students' awareness of these different uses and the constructions that go with them, and to identify any weak points in students' knowledge which need further attention.

The unit focuses primarily on ~ing forms operating as nouns (gerunds) but the use of present participles in reduced relative clauses is also recycled from Unit 5. (Participles are looked at in more detail in Unit 10.)

Anticipated problems

- Some students find the sheer variety of ~ing forms a little overwhelming. One way of overcoming this is to help them distinguish the main types. A major category here is the use of ~ing forms as nouns and to create noun phrases.

- Deciding whether to use a gerund or an infinitive is often problematic.

  Encourage students to be systematic in their approach to this by identifying regularities:

  – certain families of verbs behave in the same way (e.g. *enjoy, like, hate, detest, adore, abhor, can't bear*, etc. are all followed by a gerund).

– certain functions tend to employ a typical form (e.g. purpose is typically expressed via an infinitive – *His mother took a night job to pay his school fees*).

Procedure

a Ask students to work individually.

Then ask them to compare their answers with a partner, and monitor closely giving clues where necessary.

Check the answers as a whole class.

Ask how the examples in 5 are different from the others. Elicit that the ~ing form in 5 is not operating as a noun, i.e. it is a present participle. Some students find it helpful to have the terms/concepts *gerund* and *participle*.

b Ask students to work individually.

Then ask them to compare their answers with a partner before checking the answers as a whole class.

c Ask students to work together in pairs and discuss the reasons for their choices. Tell them to refer back to the uses in part a if they disagree.

Monitor closely pointing out the relevant information and giving clues where necessary.

Check the answers as a whole class and answer any queries on form or meaning.

6.8 # Listening

Aim

To practise listening for specific information. To transfer spoken information to other text types.

Procedure

The starting quiz is designed to introduce the topic, and to teach some of the useful vocabulary. You could add topical questions from the morning's newspapers, if you think your class would be interested. The simplest way of doing the quiz is simply to read out the questions, and students shout out the answers.

Key

a 1 verbs/expressions
Such verbs and expressions can also be followed by a noun in some cases, or nothing, e.g. *He's always enjoyed good food. It's not worth twenty dollars. It's no use (pretending you're innocent).*

2 preposition
Students should not confuse this with constructions with verb + *to* + infinitive, e.g. *I want/I have to go ...,* where *to* isn't acting as a preposition.

3 nouns
4 phrase
5 relative (Note that these examples are participles whereas the others are gerunds.)

b a 4 b 3 c 2 d 1 e 5

c 1 *gambling* is a true noun here.

2 *hiding special things* is a noun phrase, necessary due to the preposition of *before* it. (Note that *Mother was in the habit of ...* would be an expression and need an ~ing form for that reason too.)

3 *Understanding* is a gerund here used to make the noun phrase *Understanding our lack of virtue,* which is used as the subject of the verb *be.* (Note that in other contexts, *understanding* can be a true noun, e.g. *A child needs love and understanding.*)

d 1 to do/to be done 2 telling
3 dreaming 4 to sell
5 to earn 6 to please
7 cheating 8 showing/to show
9 to laugh 10 Winning

a Ask the students to study the graphs carefully. Some students may find such information difficult to absorb quickly, so do not hurry at this point.

Point out that the horizontal axes refer to days of the week, and tell them that 'today' is Tuesday (also stated on the cassette).

Elicit what has been happening in the stock exchanges in the various countries, and how the pound has been faring against other currencies. Tell them that their task is to continue the lines on the graphs. (The graphs are not in the same order as on the cassette.)

Suggested Focus Task:

F A very simple Focus Task would be to ask the students to listen once, and put the graphs in the order in which they are talked about on the cassette.

b and **c**

Give students some time to look at these before you play the cassette.

Ask students to try to complete the graphs, table and notes without stopping the tape but let them know you will play the tape at least twice. Stop the tape after each section only if you find students do not have enough time to write in the answers before the next section starts.

Key

a Quiz: 1 Great Britain 2 The dollar 3 (open answer) 4 Wall Street 5 Increase

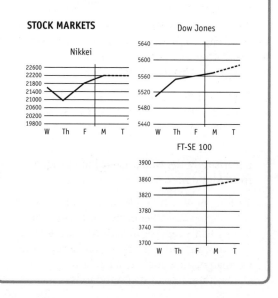

Key *(cont)*

CURRENCIES

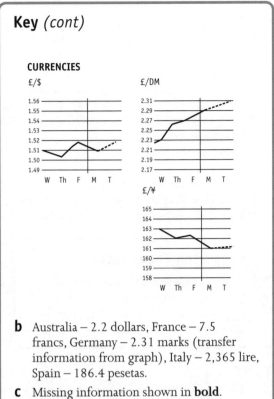

b Australia – 2.2 dollars, France – 7.5 francs, Germany – 2.31 marks (transfer information from graph), Italy – 2,365 lire, Spain – 186.4 pesetas.

c Missing information shown in **bold**.

Hassington Bank planning to **take** over Middlehampton **Building Society**. Middlehampton share price up by about **£2** – from **178p** to **368p**.

H P Lang building company made 6-monthly profit of (only) **£2.4 million** – shares **tumbled/fell** from **295p** to **190p**!

Tapescript

MALE RADIO HOST: And now just rounding up the financial news this Tuesday evening …

The Footsie One Hundred Share Index has just closed up 10 points at 3860. That's a rise of about 40 points since this time last week so things are definitely looking better.

The Dow Jones is also rallying, though trading is still in progress. At yesterday's close, it stood at 5564 and looks to be on the way up again today.

Surprisingly, the Nikkei closed unchanged from Monday.

Turning now to have a look at how the pound is faring against other currencies. It's slightly up (by half a cent) against the dollar; steady at 161 yen; and still gaining ground against the German mark – you'll need 2.31 Deutschmarks to buy a pound today.

A few tourist rates for people on the move. A pound will buy you 7.5 French francs, 186.4 Spanish pesetas, 2,365 Italian lire and 2.2 Aussie dollars.

And finally, some late-breaking news. The giant Hassington Bank has made a friendly offer to take over Middlehampton Building Society. Needless to say, the Middlehampton share price rocketed by nearly £2 to finish the day at 368 pence – up from 178 pence!

H P Lang – the building conglomerate – turned in very small six-monthly profits of £2.4 million, causing their share price to tumble from 295 pence to 190 pence at close of trading and they may slip further tomorrow.

That's it for now. Back to you, Sally.

FEMALE RADIO HOST: Thanks a lot, Gavin. Now continuing our investigation into mortgage rates … (fades) …

6.9 # Pronunciation – silent letters

Aim

To help students recognise regular and 'one-off' silent letter combinations and practise their pronunciation.

Procedure

a Put students into pairs or small groups for this task.
Check answers through open-class feedback. When you have checked answers, ask the pairs/groups to think of other combinations that produce silent letters.

b Students can first cross out the silent letters individually and then compare. Get predictions from the students before playing the tape. Play the tape, stopping after each sentence to allow individual and whole class repetition.

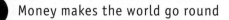

Key and tapescript

(Other possibilities not shown in the bubble in the Student's Book are shown in brackets below.)

a

wr ...	kn ...	... mb	... st(+le/en)	sc(+e/i)...
wrestling	knee	bomb	wrestling	scene
wrinkles	knock	climb	listen	science
wrist	knight	plumber	fasten	scissors
(wrong)	(knife)	(comb)	(whistle)	(scent)

... mn	... bt	gu(+a/e/i)...	... ght	... scle
solemn	debt	guarantee	knight	muscle
column	(doubt)	guide	(eight)	(corpuscle)
autumn	(subtle)	guest		
(condemn)		(guess)		

... gn	... alm	(ps ...)	(... alf)	(... alk)
design	palm	(psychic)	(half)	(talk)
(benign)	(calm)	(psychology)	(calf)	(walk)
(foreign)	(balmy)	(psalm)	(behalf)	(chalk)

(h ...)	(gn ...)	'one-offs'
(hour)	(gnat)	salmon, answer, island, receipt, sword, colonel,
(honest)	(gnome)	cupboard, iron, two etc.
(honour)	(gnash)	

b
1 Everyone condemned the rise in interest rates.
2 The building society repossessed the house as they couldn't pay the mortgage.
3 We were disappointed not to get a Christmas bonus.
4 Hugh couldn't stand the hustle and bustle of working in the Stock Exchange.
5 Bad debts completely wrecked their business.
6 Banking in the Cayman Islands might be the answer to your tax problems.
7 The bank manager was doubtful whether the scheme would work.
8 Jack was given an expensive wristwatch to soften the blow of being made redundant.
9 The plumber didn't give me a receipt and couldn't even guarantee it wouldn't break down again.
10 The manager resigned after the advertising campaign failed to attract any foreign investors.

(6.10) Review

Aim

To review selected language items from Unit 5.

Procedure

Ask students to do the task individually and then compare answers in pairs. If they have doubts, allow them to refer back to the previous unit. Check answers through open-class feedback.

Key

1 bawled 2 snug 3 Clam 4 breadline
5 eel 6 food 7 crabs 8 salt 9 sardines
10 bacon

7

Back to nature

To start you thinking

Aim

To introduce students to the theme of the unit through discovering the meanings of collocations and considering their relationship to the theme.

Procedure

a Encourage students to use their dictionaries rather than you as their first resource. Use good monolingual dictionaries if possible. Give students five to ten minutes to match up the words in bubble A with their partners in bubble B.

b Put students in pairs or, preferably, small groups of three or four and give them a time limit for their discussion.

Key

tree-felling, big game, national park, wildlife safari, whale watching, rain forests, eco-conscious politicians, rubber-tapper, natural history, dugout canoe, nesting birds, nature conservation.

Reading

Aim

To show students how much information can be packed into a short introductory summary. To understand the main points of a text. To understand detail in a text.

Procedure

a Draw the students' attention to the short introduction in the Student's Book. Ask the questions in open class, or get the students to read them in pairs and answer them together.

b Students should read these questions before reading the main text. You could then either ask the students to read the text through twice (once to confirm the questions from part a, and once to answer the questions in part b), or just once, with the students doing both exercises on the single reading. Either way, make sure they have at least ten minutes to answer the questions in part b.

c This activity should be done individually at first, with a chance later to compare answers.

Key

a 1 politician 2 young ('new generation')
3 Brazilian 4 something to save nature/ the environment/the Amazon (she is described as 'eco-conscious')
5 Yes – probably (she is an 'Amazon legend' and she's being interviewed for an international magazine)

b 1 Because she wants to stop Brazil's forests being devastated in the same way as has already happened in Europe and the USA.

2 When she had hepatitis she could no longer do the heavy physical work she had been doing before and so could start educating herself.

3 The importance of listening to others before making decisions.

4 To worry about small, local problems such as parks and flowers.

5 Yes – she has become more moderate.

c (suggested answers)

1 Acre is the state where Marina won her seat in Parliament.

2 *Farofa de paca* is her favourite meal, made of roasted rodent with cassava.

3 Three of Marina's brothers and sisters died when young.

It took Marina only three years to complete and pass all the necessary exams to enter University.

4 When Marina was fifteen, her mother died.

5 Chico Mendes was a close friend and mentor for Marina.

6 The PT is the Workers' Party, which Marina is a member of.

7 Chico Mendes was assassinated in 1988.

8 *Empates* were campaigns against tree-felling in which people formed barriers to prevent workers getting near the trees.

9 Marina has great admiration for Gandhi who fought for justice without using violence.

10 Slash-and-burn developers are Marina's main enemy – they are the people who just want to make money from the forest without worrying about the destruction they cause.

7.3 Collocations

Aim

To give students practice in recognising and understanding collocations.

Procedure

a Ask students to do the task individually and then check answers in pairs.

b Ask students to do the task individually and then check answers in pairs.

Key

a 1 whetted 2 contracted 3 realise
4 found 5 grapple 6 tooth and nail
7 carpet 8 prominence 9 dubbed
10 suffer

b 1 fight tooth and nail 2 rose to prominence
3 grapple 4 whetted ... appetite
5 contracted 6 realised 7 found 8 dubbed

7.4 Grammar – conditional sentences

Aim

This section has two aims: Firstly to consolidate students' understanding of the form and meaning of the four basic types of conditionals; 1st, 2nd, 3rd and zero. Secondly to extend their knowledge of the variety of grammar that can be used with each type of conditional, and to introduce or raise awareness of the 5th type, *mixed* conditionals.

Anticipated problems

- There are sometimes persistent problems with locating if with the conditional clause, leading to a reversal of cause and effect in the sentence,

  e.g. *I will miss the bus if I am late home.

- Students from some language backgrounds (especially speakers of Germanic languages) tend to add would/will into the conditional clause.

  *If I would have a lot of money, I would give up my job.

- Many students often wrongly assume that because the 2nd conditional uses past grammar, it refers to past time.

- Until recently, the 2nd conditional used the subjunctive, e.g. If I *were* rich ... , whereas modern English tends to use Past Simple, except in formal contexts. Students may query this point.

- Mixed conditionals can take many forms, and students may have already encountered confusing examples which seem to break the rules they have been taught.

Procedure

You could begin by writing on the board

If I was World President ...

and asking them to finish the sentence.

Then ask students to work together in pairs and write another if clause. They then exchange clauses with another pair and write answers. Monitor making corrections, and have them read some to the class.

Use their sentences, or one of your own, to check they understand *condition* and *result*.

a Ask students to work individually before comparing their answers with a partner.

b Ask students to work together in pairs, explaining the reasons for their choices. Monitor closely giving help, but don't tell them the correct answers. If they've got one wrong and it is interfering with further choices, it's helpful to tell them which answers are wrong.

Check the answers as a whole class and answer any queries on form or meaning.

Make students aware that they can expect to encounter other types of mixed conditionals. (The type presented in this unit is one of the more common and regular; it combines a 3rd conditional if clause with a 2nd conditional result clause.)

You could give the example: *If you didn't pass your exams, I can't understand how you got into university.* With stronger classes, you might ask them to write a description of its usage like those in part b.

c Ask students to work individually.

Then ask them to compare their answers with a partner. Tell them to explain their answers to each other by referring back to the uses in part b if they disagree.

Check the answers as a whole class and answer any queries on form or meaning.

Key

a 1 The article suggests that if <u>Marina Silva hadn't got hepatitis</u>, <u>she might not have become a student</u>.
                         condition   result

2 The likelihood is that <u>she wouldn't have been able to help Chico Mendes set up a Workers Party Congress</u> if <u>she hadn't gained an education</u>.
                  result   condition

3 If <u>she hadn't become involved in politics</u>, it's doubtful that <u>she'd be the 'Amazon legend' she is today</u>.
          condition   result

b FIRST d
CONDITION: present tense/aspect
RESULT: future form

SECOND a
CONDITION: past tense (or subjunctive)
RESULT: *would/should/could/might/*etc.
+ verb

THIRD e
CONDITION: Past Perfect (simple or continuous)
RESULT: *would/should/could/might/*etc.
+ *have* + past participle

MIXED c
CONDITION: Past Perfect (simple or continuous)
RESULT: *would/should/could/might/*etc.
+ infinitive form

c (Answers may vary but should be similar to the following.)

1 If it doesn't rain on Sunday, we can /'ll be able to go bird watching.

2 The wolf wouldn't have attacked if you hadn't frightened it.

3 If I knew what type of snake it is/was, I'd tell you.

4 Joe'll /'s going to be a vet if he passes his exams.

5 If we'd touched that strange plant in the jungle, we'd be in hospital now.

6 If you mate a zebra with a donkey you get a 'zedonk'!

7 If they'd seen the rhino in time, they wouldn't have crashed into it.

8 We'd be lost if I hadn't remembered to bring the map.

9 If you go swimming with crocodiles, you (usually) die!

10 If Sally spoke better Portuguese, she'd apply for that conservation job in Brazil.

7.5 Reading

Aim

To practise scanning.
To practise skimming.
To read in order to discuss personal preferences.

Procedure

a and **b**

Both these parts can be done as a competitive game, if this is suitable for your class. Ask students to cover the questions with a piece of paper. Divide the students into teams, and then read out the questions one by one. The team which finds the answer first gets a point. Make sure the students have one minute to find the answers.

c This phase gives students the chance to read the advertisements in greater detail. It is only at this stage (if at all) that you might want to look at detailed points of vocabulary.

Ask the students to read and discuss in small groups, then have a brief discussion with the whole class.

Key

a 1 E   2 £299   3 Eileen, Helen or T Coles
4 In the rainforests of Costa Rica
5 Environmentally responsible expeditions
6 Yes (they do servicing)
7 One week   8 Yes – maps   9 Madagascar
10 An anthropologist

b A, C and E=Conservation
B=Pets and wildlife   D=Photography
F=Worldwide   G=Books

7.6 Writing – leaflet

Aim

To enable students to write in a particular (but real-life) genre, in this case a leaflet.

Procedure

If you can, take some authentic leaflets into class with you. Ask the students to say what features they have in common. Answers you might get include: interesting or dramatic visuals; short paragraphs; clear and punchy style; different ways of heading and sub-heading.

If you do not have any leaflets available, use the visual in the Student's Book to elicit the same ideas. Point out the way the Causes are on one page, and the Results on another. Then elicit the various ways of breaking up the text as outlined in the Student's Book.

With the writing task itself, you may like to suggest the 'problems/solutions' division in the suggested answer below (which parallels the Causes/Results division in the Student's Book example).

If the topic of wildlife is not appropriate, here are some more ideas to choose from:

- Let's improve/clean up our city! (What's wrong? What can we do?)
- Get fit! (Why? How? Where?)
- Save energy (ten ideas)
- Stop the council closing our swimming pool! (Why? How? What can we do?)

Make sure the writing task is done in groups of three and four, preferably with a good mix of types of student within the groups.

Key

(suggested answer)

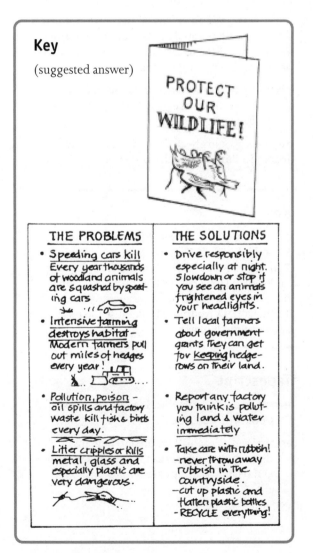

EXTRA COMMUNICATION ACTIVITY
MAY BE DONE HERE *(see page 120)*

7.7 Listening

Aim

To extract essential information from an interview.

Procedure

Start by writing *bush babies* on the board, and elicit what they might be and where they might live (Africa). Tell the students they are going to listen to an interview with someone who is going on a trip to study bush babies.

> **Suggested Focus Task:**
>
> F   Ask the students to cover Questions 2–12 with a sheet of paper, and answer just Question 1.

As always, ask the students to read the questions **before** they listen to the cassette. Make sure there are no problems with vocabulary.

Play the tape at least twice. If circumstances permit, you might like to ask students how many times they want to listen.

Students should check their answers in pairs before feeding back to the whole class.

Key

1 C 2 At night 3 It's wet 4 False
5 (Finger) nails 6 They jump/leap
7 Insects 8 Males 9 The Primate Study Group (at Brookes University) 10 To find out whether the sounds are different for different species
11 To get DNA readings 12 Because the bush babies might bite her!

Tapescript

INTERVIEWER: And um what **is** a bush baby exactly? Could you describe …?

PENNY: Well, it's actually related to humans, distantly. It's a prosimian, which is a primate and related to things like lemurs.

INTERVIEWER: Right.

PENNY: It's on a different branch of the primate family from monkeys. Monkeys have got dry noses and they've got … galagos and lemurs have got wet noses, rather like a cat or a dog. So they're distinguished by that.

INTERVIEWER: Healthy ones.

PENNY: (laughing) Yes, the healthy ones. They're small. The largest are about squirrel-size and the smallest are about as big as a hamster. And they tend to have big ears and very big eyes because, as I said, they're nocturnal and they need their big eyes in the dark. And they're distinguished as primates because they've got clasping hands and instead of claws they've got nails, like we have, finger nails and various other things like forward-looking vision and an upright posture.

INTERVIEWER: And do they … ? (Right)

PENNY: They live in trees. Different levels, depending on the species. But they live in the trees and they tend to get around not by running along the branches but by leaping and then clinging. So, well, they'll jump from one tree to the next and hang on. And they catch insects, they live on insects and they catch them with their hands, grasping the insect.

INTERVIEWER: Right. So they live in family groups, like other primates, or … ?

PENNY: Well, that's a good question. Um, apparently, I don't know, perhaps I'll be able to observe this but I'm told that the females and the young have a small territory each and that the males tend to have larger territories that overlap with different females.

INTERVIEWER: Right. And this is your first sort of trip like this.

PENNY: Yes, it is. It's very exciting.

INTERVIEWER: So who's sort of sponsoring all this?

PENNY: It's the … there's a name for it, there's an organisation, the Primate … I've forgotten the name. It's a primate group, the Primate Study Group, or something like that. Based at Oxford Uni … no, Brookes University and um the purpose is to go and try and find out different species by their sounds or to find out whether their sounds indicate that they're a different species or not. So we not only have to record them, but we also have to trap them and weigh them and measure them and take photographs of them and try and identify them and then … I believe we take hair because you can get DNA readings off their hair but we're not going to harm them, we're going to let them go again.

INTERVIEWER: Right.

PENNY: This is why I've had to have rabies jabs because I'll be handling animals and they might bite.

INTERVIEWER: Hmm. You've already had those?

PENNY: I've had one.

INTERVIEWER: Ah, it's a series.

PENNY: Mmm.

INTERVIEWER: Nasty?

PENNY: Not too bad, not too bad.

INTERVIEWER: OK. Well, thank you very much.

7.8 Hearing perception

Aim and procedure

See Introduction.

Tapescript

(*=tone)

Well yes, the healthy ones. They're small. *The largest are about squirrel-size *and the smallest are about as big as a hamster. *And they tend to have big ears and very big eyes *because, as I said, they're nocturnal and they need their big eyes in the dark. *And they're distinguished as primates *because they've got clasping hands (Right) *and instead of claws they've got nails, like we have, finger nails *and various other things like forward-looking vision and an upright posture.*

And do they … ?

They live in the trees. (Right) *Different levels, depending on the species. *But they live in the trees and they tend to get around *not by running along the branches but by *leaping and then clinging. *So, well, they'll jump from one tree to the next and hang on. *And they catch insects, they live on insects *and they catch them with their hands, grasping the insect.

7.9 Pronunciation – linking

Aim

To help students understand when linking takes place and to give them practice using it.

Procedure

Give your students plenty of chance to practise with the example. Make sure they DON'T try to put pauses between the words. Instead, you could try to get them to put pauses before the stressed sounds like this:

/it/(pause)/sɔːlwi/(pause)/zəupən/

Put students in pairs and ask them to decide how the ten examples would be pronounced. Let them say their versions before you play the tape, pausing after each phrase for correction or repetition.

Key

1 /nəʊwaɪdɪə/	2 /lʊkaʊt/
3 /suːnərɔːleɪtə/	4 /aɪjəgri/
5 /nɒtətɔːl/	6 /lʊkətʌs/
7 /nɒtɪnʌfegz/	8 /letsəksept/
9 /ɔːlɪnənɑːftənuːn/	10 /gɪvəsənaɪdiːə/

Tapescript

1 No idea.	2 Look out!
3 Sooner or later.	4 I agree.
5 Not at all.	6 Look at us.
7 Not enough eggs.	8 Let's accept.
9 All in an afternoon.	10 Give us an idea.

7.10 Review

Aim

To review selected language items from Unit 6.

Procedure

Ask students to do the task individually and then compare answers in pairs. If they have doubts, allow them to refer back to the previous unit. Check answers through open-class feedback.

Key

1 good 2 areas 3 income 4 cut 5 stock
6 notes 7 fringe 8 currencies
9 bankruptcy 10 rates

8

Shop till you drop

8.1 To start you thinking

Aim

To encourage students to think about the topic of theft from shops, so that the following text will be more accessible and they will be more able to cope with the vocabulary.

Procedure

Put students in small groups of three or four and give them a time limit of five minutes for their discussion. Get some open-class feedback and, if you know the class well, any personal confessions!

8.2 Reading

Aim

To improve the students' ability to anticipate the contents of a text, and to some extent the vocabulary, by looking at features outside the text e.g. photographs and graphics, headlines, titles and sub-titles, and layout.
To practise skimming and scanning.

Procedure

a and **b**

Do these activities in open class. The important thing is to get students guessing/ predicting the content of the article rather than the exact answers. Note that there is more work on newspaper headlines in Unit 10.

c Place a time limit on this reading. Students read on their own. Ask students to write down the answers, so you are able to check.

Key

a 2 Tesco is a British supermarket chain.

b 1 shoplifting 2 he is fed up with being caught and/or being followed around by policemen

c 1 Because he has stolen so often from their stores. 2 20,000 3 Go straight

8.3 Guessing vocabulary from textual links

Aim

To improve students' ability to guess difficult or unknown lexis by studying the links between sentences or parts of sentences.

Procedure

Put students in pairs and make sure they use the guide questions which follow each item. Do not allow the use of dictionaries. Allow ample time for discussion and justification before getting open-class feedback.

Key

1 He's famous for shoplifting, so *light-fingered* must mean 'in the habit of stealing'.

2 The previous sentence refers to being jailed, so *being inside* could mean 'inside prison/jail'.

3 He was in an open prison, so he probably had to hurry to get to the supermarket and back again, hence *nip down* probably implies speed.

4 He usually steals something, so *pinch* is probably a synonym for 'steal'.

5 He was in court, so *hearing* probably means a trial of some kind.

6 He wants to give up stealing, so *went straight* probably means something like 'lead an honest life'.

7 Probably lots of detectives, hence a *posse* would mean a group of detectives, policemen, etc. (see Unit 4 for work on this word).

8 We know he is a shoplifter, so *haul* probably refers to what he stole.

9 This is a more open answer, but one logical response would be that he does it for the excitement, so *rush of adrenalin* refers to the feeling you get when you do something risky.

8.4 Grammar – past tenses for distance from reality

Aim

This section aims to raise students' awareness of the fact that the past tense in English does not always reflect past time but instead is often used to signify unreal, imaginary or hypothetical situations. Students' attention is also drawn to typical phrases which are commonly used to introduce this function of the past tense.

Anticipated problems

- Students tend to link past and present tenses automatically to past and present time. This leads to errors like *I wish I *have* more money* and failure to recognise reference to present time when they read or hear constructions in which past grammar refers to present or general time. Similarly, students also tend to forget that an unreal situation in the past demands a shift from Past Simple and Past Continuous to Past Perfect.

- Until recently, English grammar describing unreal situations in present or general time used the subjunctive, e.g. *If I were rich* … whereas modern English tends to use Past Simple, except in formal contexts. Students may query this point.

- Students are often unaware of the difference in meaning between two common constructions:

  If only/I wish you wouldn't do that.

  If only/I wish you didn't do that.

  The first implies that the person has voluntary control over the action, whereas the second doesn't. This leads to errors like *If only/I wish we wouldn't owe so much money* which is very unnatural: while spending or borrowing money is voluntary, the state of actually being in debt at the moment of speaking is not.

Procedure

- As a lead-in, write the words *time* and *tense* on the board and ask students to translate both into their language. In many languages the two words are the same and a particular tense always refers to a particular time. This activity is helpful in drawing to students' attention the fact that the link between time and tense is not so rigid in English.

- To highlight this fact, you could recycle examples of the 1st conditional (Unit 7) and elicit that present tense in conditional clauses refers to future time.

a Ask students to work together in pairs and refer back to the reading passage to look at the sentences in context.

  - Check the answers as a whole class.
  - Many languages have subjunctives which operate as the Past Simple does here, and it may help some students to grasp the concept being studied if you point out this comparison.

b Ask students to work individually before comparing their answers with a partner.

  - Monitor closely pointing out the relevant information and giving clues where necessary.
  - Check the answers as a whole class and answer any queries on form or meaning.
  - Although the use of Past Simple to represent an unreal present is examined here in order to focus on the concept, students should be made aware that an unreal past may also involve 'back spacing' similar to that in reported speech (Unit 4):
    - in constructions with *If only/I wish* … Present Simple and Continuous change to their Past Perfect forms.
    - the 2nd conditional becomes the 3rd conditional.
    - Note that there is no 'back spacing' in constructions with *It's time* … or *… would rather* … Past forms do not become Past Perfect forms.

c Ask students to work together in pairs, explaining the reasons for their choices.

  - Monitor closely pointing out the relevant information and giving clues where necessary.
  - Check the answers as a whole class and answer any queries on form or meaning.

d Ask students to work individually.

  - Have them compare their answers with a partner and choose the best, or blend answers to create the best.

- Monitor closely pointing out errors and eliciting corrections.
- Check the answers as a whole class.

Key

a The tense in both sentences is the Past Simple.

They do not refer to past time:

It's time I **went** straight refers to present time.

I'd rather people **came** to me for advice than banned me refers to present or general time.

b Sentences 1, 4 and 7 refer to past time; the others do not.

c Most of the expressions indicate an imaginary or hypothetical situation:

2 I wish … indicates that the desired situation is not real here and now.

3 There are different possible ways of paying for goods and … would rather … indicates the preferred, not necessarily the usual method used in reality.

5 It's (about) time … means that the action has not yet happened.

6 If … signifies hypothesis.

8 If only … indicates that the desired situation is not real here and now.

d 1 … I had some money.

2 … didn't / wouldn't smoke in here.

3 … was here in Paris with me.

4 … you bought a new jumper/ got a smart suit/ dressed more smartly.

5 … had a map.

6 … didn't work so late / hard, you wouldn't be so tired in the evenings.

7 … could be with you / was there for your birthday.

8 … we went / left.

9 … didn't / wouldn't talk to each other in class.

10 … won the lottery / jackpot / £8m, what would you do / buy / spend it on?

8.5 To start you thinking

Aim

To prepare students for the following reading passage.

Procedure

Put students in groups of three or four and set a time limit of five minutes. Tell each group to appoint a secretary to note down the group's findings and decisions. At the end of the discussions, each group must report back its conclusions to the whole class.

Key
(suggested answers)

1 It has a number of different sections or departments within the same shop, often on different floors.

2 **a** department stores do not usually sell food (some do) **b** they sell more than one kind of item and are usually much larger than an ordinary shop **c** a shopping centre has a number of different shops, usually owned by different people, and connected only by being in the same place or under the same roof.

3 Probably a, c, d, e, f, g

A store guide is a map of the store, usually situated by the entrance (see 8.6).

8.6 Vocabulary

Aim

To extend and refine students' range of vocabulary in the unit topic.

Procedure

Ask students to do the task individually and then check answers in pairs. Also ask them to decide which of the wrong answers are real phrases and what they might mean.

Key

1 **c** (A secret policeman works for the secret police of a country, trying to hunt down spies, etc.)
2 **a** 3 **a** 4 **b** 5 **c** 6 **a** 7 **c** (A rest room is American English for toilet.) 8 **a**
9 **b** (A test pad is where new planes or spacecraft are tested.)

Key (cont)

10 a (The difference between a *store detective* and a *security guard* is that the former pretends to be a customer, while the latter is in uniform.)

8.7 Reading

Aim

To develop the students' awareness of coherence.

Procedure

a Start by writing the sentences about popular music from the Student's Book on the board (or by asking the students to read them in their books).

Elicit from the students that the link between the two sentences is one of *contrast* – and that there is a conjunction 'missing' – which is *but*. Elicit that a writer might leave out the conjunction to surprise the readers, or to make them think. At this point, it would be worth writing up the word *contrast* on the board.

Then students can move on to the exercise in the book. Do the first one in open class to make it clear, then ask them to do the other four in pairs.

NB: a *two-up, two-down* is a small, usually terraced house which has two rooms upstairs, and two rooms downstairs.

b In the reading text, the links between the sentences embody the ideas in section a (mostly exemplification), though there are some examples of conjunctions as well.

Point out that the numbers down the left-hand side of the text refer to sentences. Ask the students to read the complete text, underlining or highlighting words they do not understand. Students can then use dictionaries, or ask you, for the meanings of these.

The next task is to complete the organisation charts on page 82. Do the first one or two in open class as an example, then the remainder should be done in pairs and small groups. As they do this, monitor carefully, and, if they are having difficulties, bring the whole class back together to give additional help.

Stress that the actual words they use to complete the boxes are not essential – it is the ideas which are important.

Key

a 1 A **comparison**: In parts of Wales, you can buy a five-bedroomed house for £120,000, *whereas* in the south-east of England, that would just about buy you a two-up, two-down.

2 The second sentence is the **result** of the first: Many of the city's walls had been built at least a metre lower than they should have been, and *as a result*, when the rains came, a flood was inevitable.

3 The second sentence is the **cause** of the first: It was not at all surprising that the two climbers got lost, *because/since* they didn't have a map, and had never been to the place before.

4 The second sentence is an **example** of the first: Many people lost a lot of money when the bank went down. *For example*, Peter Travers, 64, from Shropshire, was forced to sell his farm and all his land.

5 The second sentence is a **conclusion** derived from the first (an **example**): Johnson's case was reported in all the papers, but only one or two included the fact that the incident happened 15 years ago. *This example shows us how* journalists often conceal important information to make their stories more sensational or controversial.

b

PARAGRAPH 1:

The main theme of paragraph 1 is:

Selfridge's changes to the look of department stores.

Sentence 1 introduces the topic by talking about an unnamed man.

Sentence 2 gives us the name of the man.

Sentences 3 and 4 give examples of the changes Selfridge made.

PARAGRAPH 2:

Paragraph 2 deals with Selfridge's in London whereas paragraph 1 deals with Selfridge's time at Marshall Field.

Sentence 5 moves the scene from the USA to Britain.

Sentence 6 shows how successful the new store was.

Sentences 7 and 8 tell us why it was such a success.

Sentence 9 expands on how Selfridge was obsessive.

Sentence 10 introduces an example of his dedication to work.

Sentence 11 continues the story.

Sentence 12 concludes the story.

PARAGRAPH 3 deals with his decline into bad and dissolute habits.

The function of sentence 13 is to contrast with what has gone before.

Sentences 14 and 15 provide examples of his new, bad behaviour.

PARAGRAPH 4 describes the results of his spending.

Sentence 16 connects back to paragraph 3 by saying how much he spent.

Sentence 17 uses the word 'it' to link to sentence 16 ('it' refers to the $8 million).

Sentences 18, 19 and 20 all describe how he lost everything (his position, his money and his house).

8.8 Writing – using examples to create coherence

Aim

To improve students' non-linguistic linking (='coherence').
To get students structuring their written discourse in a more fluid way, and without the overt use of discourse markers.

Procedure

Start by giving the students the title of the text they are going to write, and ask the whole class for ideas. Then ask them to study the drawing on page 83 for a few minutes, and clear up any queries about vocabulary.

Ask the students to group the examples in the illustration into similar types. They then use the chart on page 83 of the Student's Book to write the final piece. This should be done in pairs or small groups. Students then write the four paragraphs, in class or for homework.

As far as correction is concerned, we would advise feedback on the organisational elements as the prime aim, rather than more 'local' problems of grammar, punctuation etc. Students preparing for an exam where the accuracy is important will need more detailed feedback, however. See the Introduction for general points about correction. For more ideas and tips on techniques of correcting written English, see *Correction* by Bartram and Walton (Language Teaching Publications, 1991).

Key

(suggested answer)

The next time you go shopping at your local supermarket, take a careful look round. Because one of the reasons that stores like this achieve such high sales is that every aspect of the way they look, and the way they are arranged, is carefully designed to do just one thing – make you buy!

Supermarkets organise the space in which the customers move in such a way as to maximise sales. A supermarket entrance will usually be on the left side of the building, because this (apparently) increases customer attention. The aisles are much broader than they used to be: customers go slower down wide aisles, and buy more as a result. The disposition of the goods is changed every so often so that customers have to search out their favourites, and in doing so walk past other goods.

In fact, *where* the products are situated is an important factor in how well they sell. Goods sell best at the end of the aisle, where the customer slows down to go round the corner. Items which are at eye level sell better. Basic foodstuffs like tea or bread are usually put at the back of the store, so that the customers have to go past – and hopefully, buy – more expensive goods to get to them.

Finally, the way a store *looks* is important in the image that a store creates. Displays of fruit, vegetables, flowers and houseplants are placed immediately inside the entrance to promote an appealing image of 'greenness' and freshness. The colours of the shop are chosen carefully – at present green is in fashion. Large displays are created, because it has been proved that people buy more from large displays than from smaller ones.

EXTRA COMMUNICATION ACTIVITY MAY BE DONE HERE *(see page 121)*

8.9 Pronunciation – word-class pairs

Aim

To raise students' awareness of word-class pairs. To encourage students to produce the word-class pairs in a controlled situation.

Procedure

a Because the position of the stress depends on the **meaning** of the words, students need to listen to the adverts carefully before they attempt to work out stress rules.

F

Suggested Focus Task:

On a first listening, students should answer the question in the Student's Book.

If you wish, you could ask the students to answer more detailed questions for each advert, such as:

Advert 1: What is the name of the shop?
Where is it?
How much are apples? etc.

Advert 2: What is the main advantage of shopping at Bicester Shopping Village?

Advert 3: What do you think was sitting on Chandler's desk?

Advert 4: What adjective is used to describe Southern Jeans?

Advert 5: What is the name and address of the security company?

Advert 6: Who was the film made by?
What certificate is it?

b This part should be done in pairs.

c Be prepared for a bit of noise in this part! The students should say the words before listening to the tape, which should be used as a check.

d This is the most important part of the whole section, because it is fairly easy for students to reproduce the stress patterns when saying individual words, but much more difficult for them to do so in connected speech.

These dialogues are obviously fairly artificial, so you might like to add a humorous element. Get students to 'ham it up' a bit, saying their parts comically or exaggeratedly.

Ask the students to read the dialogues silently at first, paying attention to the pronunciation of the words from parts a–c.

Then they should read the dialogue out loud in pairs. Monitor carefully. Try to interrupt them as little as possible. Encourage self- and peer-correction. Only correct the target words.

Finally, choose different pairs to read out one dialogue each to the whole class.

Key

a 1 a greengrocer's 2 a 'Shopping Village'
3 a floor-cleaner 4 jeans 5 a burglar alarm
6 a film

Stress as follows:

○	○
produce (n)	subject (adj)
○	○
object (v)	suspect (v)
○	○
perfect (adj)	rebel (n)
○	○
increase (n)	record (adj)
○	○
convict (n)	contract (n)
○	○
escort (v)	desert (n)

b The basic rule: when it is a verb, the stress is on the second syllable, whereas a noun or an adjective have the stress on the first. (There are exceptions, such as *purchase* – stress always on the first, or *resort* – stress always on the second.)

c

○	○	○
suspect	perfect	increase
○	○	○
conduct	protest	desert
○	○	○
upset	insult	convert
○	○	○
abstract	exports	present

d Dialogue 1: *increase* – stress on second; *produce* – stress on first; *protest* – stress on second

Dialogue 2: *conduct* – stress on second; *object* – stress on second; *record* – stress on first; *Rebel Rebel* – stress on first (though it could be on the second)

Dialogue 3: *present* – stress on first; *perfect* – stress on first

Dialogue 4: *convict* – stress on first; *objects* – stress on first

Tapescript

ADVERTISEMENT 1: Do you miss the good old days when fruit and veg were really fresh? Well, at Bolton's of Ipswich, we can promise you the freshest produce in town. And look at these prices. Braeburn apples 80 pence a pound, fresh British strawberries one pound a punnet, Spanish broccoli 52 pence a pound. Bolton's of Ipswich – at 18 Queen Street, Ipswich. All prices subject to change without notice.

ADVERTISEMENT 2: Do you object to paying inflated prices for designer goods? Well, come to Bicester Shopping Village, where you can find top names in fashion, interior design and furniture at more than 20% off the High Street price! Bicester Shopping Village – it's a whole new shopping experience.

ADVERTISEMENT 3: When Chandler came back to his apartment, he noticed that something was out of place. The floor was unnaturally clean and shiny. He thought he knew who to suspect. He opened the door to his office … slowly. A sweet perfume hit him. Sitting on his desk was the culprit. Bitter. Lemony. Tangy. His floors would never be dirty again.

New Spliff floorshine. Perfect for floors. Perfect for you. From all good stores and supermarkets.

ADVERTISEMENT 4: Ah always thought of myself as an outsahder, y'know … thrown aht ah school, spent long years on the road, bit of a hobo, yah know? Bin travelling from town to town. One thing ah never changed, that's mah Southern Jeans, cos they TOUGH, man, y'know? They tell you sumping baht a man.

Southern Jeans. For the rebel in you.

ADVERTISEMENT 5: Theft and burglary from private houses is on the increase. Last year, one out of every six people suffered a break-in of some kind at home. Crime is at a record high. Make sure YOUR house is safe from burglars by installing the new Philatronic 2000 alarm system. Available from Nine oh nine Security, Bath Street, Edinburgh.

ADVERTISEMENT 6: He was an ex-convict looking for a reason to live. **She** was an artist with a contract on her head. His job: to escort her from Washington DC to a courthouse in Texas. Her job: to stay alive for six more days.

A Justin Rivera film. *Desert Runner*. Certificate 15. In all good cinemas now.

8.10 ## Review

Aim

To review selected language items from Unit 7.

Procedure

Ask students to do the task individually and then compare answers in pairs. If they have doubts, allow them to refer back to the previous unit. Check answers through open-class feedback.

Be sure to elicit from the students the meanings of the phrases once they have worked out the pairings from the chart.

Key

nature conservation, natural history, to grapple with a crisis, to fight tooth and nail, to found a party or organisation, air pollution, tree-felling, national park, wildlife safari, big game

NB: there will be other phrases that could be produced by the chart (e.g. wildlife conservation)

Lessons in life

9.1 To start you thinking

Aim

To introduce students to the theme of the unit through reflection and discussion.

Procedure

Put the students in groups of four for the discussion. If you have a motivated class, set a time limit of ten minutes. Get some open-class feedback from the different groups. You may like to add some comments of your own.

Note: 'Education is what survives when what has been learnt has been forgotten' is a quotation by B F Skinner, the famous behaviourist. He seems to be saying that 'education' comes from within the person and stays, whereas 'learning' is external and disappears over time.

9.2 Reading

Aim

To understand the gist of different paragraphs in a text.

Procedure

Give students as much time as they need to read carefully. It might be worth giving them a couple of pre-reading questions before they read the text.

There are two ways of dealing with the matching activity. Either, ask the students to match the nine headings to the six paragraphs as they go along. (Don't forget to tell them that they only need to use six, and that three will remain unused.) Or, ask them to read the six paragraphs without seeing the nine headings first, and to suggest a short heading (no more than six words) for each one – this is a more active exploration of the text, and it also tests their productive (writing) skills more. After they have suggested six headings, they read through the list of nine to find the best match.

In either case, make sure they do the exercise in pairs, with a feedback session in the whole class. Ask for justifications.

Key

1 E 2 I 3 F 4 D 5 A 6 G

9.3 Reading – interpretation

Aim

To practise finding factual information in a text.
To practise interpreting the writer's ideas.

Procedure

This exercise requires a more detailed reading than 9.2, so make sure the students have plenty of time for it – at least ten minutes.

The students should work individually at first, then compare answers in pairs. Where there are no clear answers (e.g. in 4) the important thing is that students try to justify their answers from what they read in the text.

Key

1 Parents and adults who are involved with children.

2 Because they are not given enough time to think about an answer by adults.

3 No – (s)he seems to be a scientist or teacher of science. ('I once visited a class of seven-year-olds to talk about science as a career.')

4 No clear evidence – in fact the writer is a woman – Mary Budd Rowe.

5 False – she thinks the way it is often taught **makes** it boring.

6 Such a phrase can show a child the conversation is over rather than encouraging further discussion.

7 She would tell them to involve pupils more, let them ask questions, give them more time to think, not frustrate their natural curiosity with the boring transfer of information.

8 Her ideas seem to be much closer to the original idea of 'education'.

9.4 Vocabulary

Aim

To lead students to an understanding of more difficult vocabulary in the reading text.

Procedure

Put students in pairs for this task. Encourage them to discuss and justify their answers. Get some open-class feedback to check answers at the end.

Key

1 leading question 2 barrage of questions
3 jargon 4 magnifying glass 5 misconception
6 cause and effect 7 hands on
8 keep the ball rolling 9 drudgery 10 mould

9.5 Reading

Aim

To scan information presented in different formats.
To use information from graphics to complete a text.

Procedure

a Point out that information presented graphically is as important as text (and is increasingly to be found in public examinations).

Ask the students to study the different tables for a few minutes. Then ask them to work individually to answer the questions. They should do this quickly – you might set a time limit – and then feed back to the whole class.

b Point out before they begin this part that they may need to present the information in a different way in order to complete the text (e.g. by changing percentages to fractions).

Key

a 1a C 1b D 1c A 1d B 2 Italy 3 8%
b 1 quarters 2 females 3 1970/71
4 ten 5 human sciences 6 Japan
7 5.3 8 1994 9 fifth 10 twice

9.6 COLLOCATIONS AND LEARNER TRAINING

Aim

To improve students' dictionary reference skills, to extend their knowledge of collocation and to use a vocabulary recording technique already presented in this book.

Procedure

a Put students in pairs or groups and tell them to use dictionaries if necessary. Remind students that as well as crossing out the incorrect collocations, they should try to provide the correct expression. Get open-class feedback to check answers.

b Students may remain in their pairs for this task. After checking answers, encourage students to do other grids for **course** or **lesson(s)** etc.

c Ask students to do the task individually and then check answers in pairs.

Key

a Only the incorrect collocations with corrected alternatives are included.

1 bed and board=boarding **school**/ one sex=single sex **school**

2 **school** apparatus=**school** equipment

3 **school** pupil (*school* is not necessary before *pupil*)/colleague=mate or friend

4 assist=attend or go to **school**

5 game=play **school**

6 No incorrect collocations

7 obligatory/mandatory=compulsory **education**

8 supplementary=further/higher **education**

9 make=have **lessons**

10 make=follow/take **a course**

---

b Below are some possible grids for **school** & **education** with further suggestions shown in **bold**.

Verbs	Describing words	Keyword	Words that come after
attend go to drop out of **leave** **start**	boarding co-educational single-sex private public/state **secondary/high** **comprehensive**	school	report system year mate friend **playground** **bus**
continue **abandon** enrol in	higher further compulsory adult full/part-time **secondary** **basic**	education	**secretary** (political) course system

c 1 Comprehensive 2 friends/pals/chums/mates 3 public 4 days 5 education
6 leaving age 7 child 8 education

(9.7) Writing – adding detail

Aim

To encourage students to add colour to their writing by using detail.

Procedure

Ask the students to read through the whole text as it stands on the page of the Student's Book. Ask what is wrong with it (it is dull). Explain that their job is to add interesting (not necessarily true) detail to liven it up. Do the first one as an example:

> *When I was 6 years old I went to a primary school, or scuola elementare as it's called in Italy. The name of the school was 'Carlo Ederle' and, luckily for me, it was only about 300 metres from my flat so I could walk there in a few minutes. It was quite a big school with about 400 pupils.*

Students should complete the task individually. If appropriate, gather in the completed versions, read them out to the class, and ask them to guess who wrote which. Alternatively, ask students to vote on which text supplies the funniest/most interesting detail.

(9.8) Grammar – *any* and *some*

Aim

To get students to think about the uses of *any* and *some* and to work out for themselves that the old rule 'any in questions and negatives and *some* in affirmatives' is less than adequate.
To make students aware that in many cases both *some* and *any* are possible but carry different meanings and therefore need to be chosen in relation to context and intended meaning.

Anticipated problems

● Some difficulties may arise regarding the concept that *any* can refer to the whole or totality of something if students over-generalise the application of this idea. In:

I haven't brought any of my books/I haven't brought some of my books

the first means that all of my books are absent while the second means that only some are absent. However, in:

*I've brought all of my books/*I've brought any of my books*

the sense of totality represented by the first cannot be expressed via the second. It is important that students clearly understand the difference between *any* and *all*, and that *all* is generally used in normal affirmative contexts (see part a).

- Both *some* and *any* are used in many set expressions where their meaning may be different from those here, and students may have already encountered particular uses which do not seem to agree with the general rules presented here.

Procedure

Write the well-known rule: '*Any* in questions and negatives and *some* in affirmatives' on the board, but leave gaps for *some* and *any* and elicit these from the class. Then draw students' attention to the two examples from the reading passage 9.2, and ask if they follow the rule. (The second breaks it.) Point out the conclusion that we need more effective rules.

a Ask students to read through the new rules and check that they understand them before moving on to the exercise. They may have difficulty seeing *any* in terms of *whole* or *unlimited*, and if they do you could use the examples:

I don't like any of the subjects at school.

(Name any one, or more, of them and the fact is that I dislike it. I dislike all of them.)

I'd be happy to get into any of the colleges I've applied to.

(If I'm accepted by just one, or more, of them – I'll be happy. None of them would be a disappointment, all are capable of making me happy.)

For the matching, ask students to work together in pairs, explaining the reasons for their choices.

Monitor closely pointing out the relevant information and giving clues where necessary.

Check the answers as a whole class and answer any queries on form or meaning.

b Ask students to work together in pairs. Tell them to explain their answers to each other by referring back to the uses in part a if they disagree.

Check the answers as a class.

c Ask students to work individually.

Then ask them to compare their answers with a partner. Tell them to explain their answers to each other by referring back to the uses in part a if they disagree.

Key

a 1 A 2 B 3 C, D 4 C 5 D 6 D 7 A 8 B
  9 A 10 A, B 11 A 12 D (a request)

b 1 Both possible: *any*=all classical music; *some*=only Bach or Puccini, for example.

2 Both possible: *any*=I'm not sure if you have any, or that you will give them to us; *some*=I'm fairly sure you've got some that you'll give to us.

3 Both possible: *any*=I really don't know; *some*=I suspect you probably did.

4 Only *any*; the necessary information is wholly absent.

5 Only *some*; a limited amount.

6 Only *any*; all school kids know so you have an unlimited choice of which to ask.

7 Only *any*; all his answers are impossible to understand.

8 Both possible: *any*=all, *some*=only buildings by Frank Lloyd Wright or Le Corbusier, for example.

9 Only *some*; I am sure of their existence.

10 Only *some*; I am sure of their existence, I expect the answer to be *yes*, and it is a request.

c 1 any (expected answer is *no*)

2 some (they are known to exist)

3 some (I didn't go to a limited number)

4 some (expected answer is *yes*)

5 any (*any* means *all*)

9.9 LISTENING

Aim

To practise listening for specific information.
To practise interpreting a listening text.

Procedure

> **Suggested Focus Task:**
>
> Answer these two questions:
>
> 1 What are the first names of the three people interviewed?
>
> (F) 2 Which one
>   a says their school was brilliant?
>   b talks about their first day at school?
>   c feels their teachers had a narrow view of life?

As usual, make sure the students read the questions before you play the cassette. Play the cassette at least twice.

Students should discuss their answers to the questions in pairs and small groups, before feeding back to the whole class.

Key

1 Turner.   2 A small one in a little village.
3 To prepare for life, be responsible for yourself and find inner happiness.
4 They were 'brilliant' – some are still her 'friends'.   5 That they are bad for pupils and can leave them 'damaged'.   6 They just wanted pupils to pass exams, they didn't make subjects interesting for pupils.   7 It didn't seem to have any relevance to real life.
8 He's a writer/ journalist.   9 Claire ('I made some really close friends, boys and girls and teachers').   10 Chris.

Tapescript

PERSON A – THOMAS

INTERVIEWER: So, what do you remember about your school days?

THOMAS: What do you mean? Good things or bad things?

INTERVIEWER: Either. Just anything that stands out in your mind.

THOMAS: Um … well. I'll never forget my first day at secondary school. It was quite a trauma for me as I'd been at a little village school up until then, in a class of ten kids, all nice and cosy really. And then all of a sudden there I was at 'big school', surrounded by hundreds of, what seemed to me at the tender age of eleven, very big boys! In the classroom there were about thirty of us. The teacher was very strict and I soon found out I was no longer called Tommy but Turner TJ – form 1B! I was in a state of shock, I suppose. I didn't really talk all day, except to say 'Yes, sir!'

PERSON B – CLAIRE

INTERVIEWER: Can you tell me something about your school days, Claire?

CLAIRE: Yeah sure! They were great! Really the 'best days of my life'. As you know, I went to Summerhill, which is, like, tooootally different from any other school. The main idea is that you go to school to prepare for life, be responsible for yourself and find inner happiness and NOT to be pushed around by small-minded teachers who just want you to pass lots of exams so their school looks good. I mean, places like that can leave a person damaged for life! No, Summerhill was brilliant. You don't have to go to lessons but you can if you want – with brilliant teachers too. You spend your time doing what you think is important. You don't have to take any exams. Mind you, I did and so did most of my friends. I made some really close friends, boys and girls and teachers! I'm still in touch with most of them now.

PERSON C – CHRIS

INTERVIEWER: How do you rate your school education, Chris? Did it prepare you for life?

CHRIS: That's a good question. Um … I think the short answer is a definite 'No!' Looking back, it seems incredible that there were never any discussions about careers after school. I suppose that's because the teachers had such a narrow view of life – working to the curriculum and getting pupils to pass exams. None of what I was taught seemed to have any relevance to real life. I once asked a teacher what geometry was for. He said it taught one how to solve problems. If, instead, he'd told me the word came from the Greek 'ge', the earth, and 'metron', a measure, and that the meaningless triangles I was asked to juggle with formed the basis of geographical exploration, astronomy and navigation, the subject would have immediately become much more romantic, exciting and, well, you know, appealing. So, when I left school I didn't have the faintest idea about what I wanted to do. I eventually drifted into writing and journalism based initially on my diaries of my travels around Europe after I left school with nowhere to go!

> **EXTRA COMMUNICATION ACTIVITY MAY BE DONE HERE** *(see page 122)*

(see page 122)

(9.10) ## Review

Aim

To review selected language items from Unit 8.

Procedure

Ask students to do the task individually and then compare answers in pairs. If they have doubts, allow them to refer back to the previous unit. Check answers through open-class feedback.

Key

1 light-fingered 2 inside 3 nip 4 trolley
5 pinched 6 straight 7 claimed 8 checkout
9 fitting room 10 store detective

Read all about it!

10.1 To start you thinking

Aim

To introduce students to the theme of the unit through comparison between the British press and that of other countries.

Procedure

Put the students in small groups of three or four. Give groups a time limit of five to ten minutes. Check answers through open-class feedback.

Key

(suggested answers)

1 In Britain, the words *tabloid* and *broadsheet* technically refer to the size of the newspaper but they are now used (especially *tabloid*) to refer to the content: tabloid papers tend to focus on sensational stories about royalty and TV/film personalities, crime stories, sport and (less and less) stories about social issues. Most of the stories are about Britain. When they do feature serious stories, they tend to take a populist or sensational angle on them. Broadsheet papers tend to feature more political news, more foreign news, more analytical or discursive articles. However, the difference is getting smaller as broadsheets in Britain feature more and more stories about crime and royalty.

2 Open answers.

3 Open answers, but students often find the colloquial language and obscure cultural references ('Tory admits dole figures are a fiddle') of the tabloids to be more baffling.

4 Probably a tabloid (in fact from the *Mirror*). It has a banner headline and the content is rather trivial.

10.2 Reading

Aim

To predict the content of a text from headlines. To compare the vocabulary, style and organisation of articles from two British newspapers.

Procedure

Note that 10.5 has a further activity which looks at the formality or informality of some of the vocabulary in these passages.

a This part should be done with the whole class. Ask the students to study the headlines (ask them to cover the texts at this point). Elicit answers to the three questions. Apart from *joyriders*, do not pre-teach any vocabulary, as the post-reading activities deal with this.

b Stress that the students should read quickly – discourage use of dictionaries, or any detailed work on vocabulary at this point. Students should work on their own, with a short time given over to comparing answers in pairs.

After feeding back on the answers, tell the students that Article 1 comes from the *Mirror* (a tabloid) and Article 2 from the *Guardian* (a broadsheet).

c These questions should be answerable without too much work on the vocabulary. Try to avoid explaining words which come up in part d, but any other words which prevent global understanding could be explained at this stage.

d Students work through the two columns of words in pairs and small groups and match up similar items. Point out that these are not necessarily synonyms – they are simply the different lexical items that the papers have chosen to express the same idea.

e This discussion could take place in fours but make sure that you have a whole-class feedback.

NB: one difference between the two accounts is that the *Mirror* version has the policeman as Simon Waddington while the *Guardian* has him as Nick Waddington. See if your students notice this!

Key

a 1 *joyriders* are people (usually young boys) who steal cars and drive them around at speed for fun.

2 (suggested) Two children have stolen a car, driven it fast, and crashed it.

3 (suggested) the second headline was in the tabloid – mainly because of the size of the headline, and perhaps the slightly more dramatic tone.

b (suggested answers)
- the boys were very young
- they nearly died and the police acted bravely to save them
- the whole story happened in the middle of the night when the rest of the family were asleep

c (Some of the answers to these questions are interpretations rather than facts, and you should accept different interpretations provided they are well justified.)

1 Open answer.

2 The Mirror: a, d, f, g, i; The Guardian: b, c, e, h.

3 The Mirror's inclusions tend to be more emotive – the speed of the vehicle, the fact that the eight-year-old is too young to be prosecuted, younger and younger children are involved in crime; the *Guardian's* tend to focus more on the police – what they said, what they're going to do.

4 They both put the age of the youngsters right at the beginning (and in the headline). They both quote the father. They both tell the story of the chase in some detail. They both tell us what injuries the youngsters suffered.

5 In the *Mirror's* version, the father's comments come earlier, but apart from slight differences in the order in which the information comes, the basic structure is very similar:

Age of youngsters
Police pulling them out
Injuries

Basic story
Father's comments
Police comments
Witness's comments
Legal implications

You could argue that the *Mirror*, by putting the father's comments earlier, sees it more from the children's point of view, whereas the *Guardian* is more interested in the police's side, but the difference is small.

6 Open answers.

d 1j, 2b, 3l, 4a, 5g, 6f, 7i, 8d, 9k, 10m, 11h, 12c, 13e

e (suggested answers)

1 the *Mirror* chooses more dramatic vocabulary (*ploughed* rather than *crashed*, flames *engulfing* the car, *spot* rather than *see*, although arguably *gave chase* is more dramatic than *trail*)

2 the *Guardian* tends to choose a more formal alternative (*stolen* rather than *nicked*, *abandoned* rather than *dumped*, *police officers* rather than *PC/WPC*)

3 the *Mirror's* vocabulary is more judgmental (*tearaways* rather than *lads*)

4 the *Guardian* chooses words which are slightly more obscure (*derelict* rather than *disused*) or precise (*erratically*)

The overall effect is that the *Mirror* tends to choose dramatic, emotional, colloquial language (perhaps because it is trying to impersonate the way it thinks its readers speak); the *Guardian* a more objective, more precise, and less emotive tone (perhaps it is trying to impersonate the way it thinks its readers speak!).

But what is interesting is that the articles are actually very **similar** (perhaps because the information has simply been given out by the police to the newspapers?), which rather negates the common assumption that tabloids and broadsheets write their articles in very different ways.

(10.3) Vocabulary

Aim

To make students more aware of 'lexical variation' in order to avoid repetition and increase reader interest.

Procedure

a Put students in pairs or small groups for this task and encourage discussion. Check answers through open-class feedback.

b Put students in pairs or small groups for this task and encourage discussion. Check answers through open-class feedback.

c Put students in pairs or small groups and ask them to go through the text, underlining words or phrases which are repetitions of something which has gone before. Check answers through open-class feedback. Once they have identified what needs changing, ask them to come up with alternatives. (Point out that Ealing is a part of west London.)

Key

a 1 *the ten-year-old boy* refers to *Taylor Touchstone*
2 *fire* refers to *blaze* 3 *place* refers to *Salzburg*
4 *the astonished woman* refers to *Sue Phillips*
5 *a pilot* refers to *Luis Eduardo Iglesias*; *chopper* is also a lexical variation on *helicopter*
6 *a young German couple* refers to *Anneliese and Axel Probst*

b Article 1: joyriders, the driver and his passenger; the step brother, the two tearaways; the youngsters, the children; car, Vauxhall Cavalier, the F reg Cavalier; police, PC/WPC.

Article 2: car, vehicle, the Vauxhall Cavalier; building, a derelict pub; the boys, the kids; constable, officers.

c (suggested answers) Words or phrases which could be changed and suggested variations (in **bold**):

line 4 Blake > **The executive**;
line 5 muggers > **delinquents/thugs**;
line 7 Blake > **the businessman**;
line 9 Help > **Aid/Assistance**;
line 11 street > **road**;
line 11 the street > **over**;
line 12 muggers > **thieves**;
line 13 Ealing > **This part of London**;
line 16 muggers > **criminals**;
line 17 Edith > **the (courageous) old lady**;
line 18 help > **look out for/assist**;
line 20 incident > **case**;
line 22 muggers > **teenagers**;
line 23 Police > **The authorities**;
line 24 incidents > **attacks**;
line 24 Ealing > **the west London suburb**;
line 25 knives > **weapons**.

(10.4) Grammar – using participles

Aim

This section aims to extend students' awareness and command of different uses of participles with the focus on:

- the use of present and past participles:
  - in their familiar roles of forming the continuous and perfect aspects, and in passive constructions.
  - as adjectives.
  - to form adjectival clauses. (Where these adjectival phrases follow the noun, they generally act as reduced relative clauses.)
  - in forming object complements, particularly with verbs of sense (*see, hear, smell*, etc.), to give information about the actions of the object of the sentence.
  - in forming adverbial clauses describing why, when or how something happened.

- the use of perfect participles in forming adverbial clauses describing why or when something happened.

Anticipated problems

- The fact that *be* is used as an auxiliary verb in both passive and continuous constructions can sometimes lead to confusion. In sentences which are both passive and continuous, students tend to drop one of the two necessary auxiliaries, e.g. *They <u>are being</u> interviewed by the police* becomes **They <u>being</u> interviewed...*

- Although there are many true adjectives derived from participles, students should be warned that participles themselves are not always reliable as adjectives. Their unpredictable word order is the main cause of difficulties. Some occur only after the noun, causing errors like **Police kept a file on the investigated people*, while others can occur before or after the noun but with a change to meaning.

- Problems with adverbial clauses arise when students forget that the subject of the adverbial clause is normally the same as in the main clause, e.g. **Smashing the window, the glass cut the burglar's hand*, giving the impression that the glass broke the window.

Procedure

a Ask students to work together in pairs, explaining the reasons for their choices. Monitor closely, pointing out the relevant information and giving clues where necessary.

Check the answers as a whole class and answer any queries on form or meaning.

Point out that participles used as adjectives can be used to form reduced relative clauses, e.g.

The people questioned saw nothing.
The man driving was an ex-policeman.
The man talking to the judge is a lawyer.
The woman arrested by the police has been released.

b Ask students to work individually before comparing their answers with a partner. Monitor closely pointing out the relevant information and giving clues where necessary.

Check the answers as a whole class and answer any queries on form or meaning.

Explain that the subject of the adverbial clause is normally the same as in the main clause. You could use the example:

*Smashing the window, the glass cut the burglar's hand.

This gives the impression that the glass broke the window! The sentence should be

Smashing the window, the burglar cut his hand on the glass.

c Ask students to work together in pairs, referring back to the information in parts a and b if they disagree.

Monitor closely pointing out the relevant information and giving clues where necessary.

Check the answers as a whole class.

If students have used *after* in their answers to 2, 3, 6, ask them to rewrite them using perfect participles.

Key

a 1 a   2 b   3 a   4 a, b   5 b   6 a, c   7 c

b 1 how (=The prisoner twisted… and in this way…); present participle

2 why (= She was surrounded by the police and so…); present and past participle together − this construction is called a *passive participle*

3 when (=Before they left…); present participle

4 when (=They broke into the vault and then…); active

5 why (= Because she had been robbed…); passive

c 1 The watchman saw the vandals smashing all the windows in the sports pavilion.

2 Having destroyed the evidence, the crooks felt confident of getting away with their crime. / After destroying the evidence, the crooks felt confident of getting away with their crime.

3 Having been caught with stolen documents, the minister was forced to resign. / After being caught with stolen documents, the minister was forced to resign.

4 The sniffer dogs could smell the explosives hidden in the luggage.

5 Sobbing uncontrollably, the suspect insisted that she was innocent. / The suspect sobbed uncontrollably, insisting that she was innocent.

6 Having been handcuffed, the rioter was unable to resist arrest. / After being hand-cuffed, the rioter was unable to resist arrest.

7 Everyone could hear the police sirens getting closer!

8 Thinking he was likely to be captured, the escaped convict hid in a barn for six days.

(10.5) Listening

Aim

To practise listening to a story, and order the main events.
To interpret informal language and slang in a listening text.

Procedure

a The students will probably be familiar with the idea that words can be formal or informal in style. The idea of 'neutrality' may be new to them. Discuss some of the words in the list in open class before letting students work through individually.

b Don't spend too much time on this. It is not a story-telling exercise, but a preparation activity for the listening. Five minutes should be enough.

Then play the tape once only.

Suggested Focus Task:

F Listen out for the differences between your own predicted story and the one on the cassette.

c Ask the students to read through the statements. Although they will have heard the tape by now, do not discuss the answers at this stage.

Play the tape through a second time. The students should discuss the answers in pairs, and then feed back to the whole class.

d Play the tape and ask students to write down the meaning as the words come up in the passage.

Key

a (suggested answers)

Informal: *sneaked out, nicked, lads, kids, out cold*
Formal: *offences, police officers, vehicle, prosecuted, internal injuries, sustained, thereby*
Neutral: *escaped, minor, father, witness*

NB: *minor* tends to be used more in legal English than in everyday speech.

c 1 T 2 T 3 F 4 T 5 F 6 F 7 T

d (suggested answers)
(N=neutral, F=formal)

2 starving – hungry (N)

3 daylight robbery – much too expensive/costs too much (N)

4 yucky – disgusting, horrible (N)

5 make a fuss – complain (N)

6 stuff – material (N)

7 know what I mean? – do you understand what I mean? (N)

8 hacked off – angry (N)

9 she's **down** two Supahoops – she has two Supahoops fewer (N)

10 her **little** brother – younger (N)

11 he's laughing his head off! – he's laughing very much, with great energy (N)

12 the thing is – the point is (N)

13 week in week out – every week (N)

14 **get** her another packet – obtain (F)

15 better still – even better (N)

16 dosh – money (N)

Tapescript

MAN: …well, anyway, I was out with the kids, y'know, took 'em for a walk, y'know, like, in the buggy, and they was howling for

something to eat, so we moseys into the corner shop, y'know, in Wood Green, and they're starving, y'know, so we get these Supahoops off the shelves, y'know, 33p each – daylight robbery, and well we get out of the shop, and the little nippers just rip open the bag and then the girl starts screaming 'Daddy, Daddy! there's yucky yucky,' but of course they're back in the buggy by now, and it's too late, I can't be bothered to go back in and make a fuss, so we're in the park, and I look in the packet, and there's this… I dunno how to describe it really, piece of crispy stuff, like fried stuff, with two black bits in it, like someone's dropped a used sticky plaster in the mix… God, I came over all funny when I saw it, cos it looked sorta DEFORMED, know what I mean? like someone's finger in there… y'know what I mean?

Anyway, 'course the kid's really hacked off, 'cos she's down two Supahoops, y'know, and her little bruvver's got a packet too, but 'e ain't got any yucky bits in 'is, has he? So 'e's laughing 'is 'ead orf! … and the thing is, y'know, we've been going down the shops, getting a packet of Supahoops every Sunday for YEARS, y'know, week in week out, and they've always been perfect… never been anything wrong before…

… so I promise her, like, I'll send a letter to Supahoops Limited, or whatever, and get 'er another packet, or better still, get some dosh from them, 'nuff to pay for a couple o' beers down the Pig 'n' Whistle, eh??? buy her a little dolly to make it up to her, y'know what I mean?… fair enough…

EXTRA COMMUNICATION ACTIVITY MAY BE DONE HERE *(see page 123)*

(10.6) Writing – choosing correct register

Aim

To enable students to choose the correct register for writing tasks.

Procedure

a Elicit from the students that the storyteller in 10.5 is going to write a letter of complaint to the crisp company. Write the words and phrases from the Student's Book on the board and ask students to say why they would be inappropriate in such a letter, and how they would re-phrase them.

b Revise the three categories of *formal*, *informal* and *neutral* language the students studied in 10.5. Point out that language that is too formal can be as offensive as colloquial language, because it can sound as if you are making fun of the other person.

Ask students to read through the letter in pairs. They should find the inappropriate words and phrases, suggest alternatives and then feed back to the whole class.

Key

a 1 (In fact), it would be difficult to describe it (accurately).
   2 as if
   3 a long time, many years
   4 never had any problems previously
   5 compensate her for it

b These answers are open to interpretation – each writer has their own style, and what may appear too casual to one person may seem perfectly all right to another. Feel free to disagree!

   1 *just* is more appropriate for a short note
   2 *purchased* might be thought too formal – why not use *bought*?
   3 *a couple of* – *two* (too informal)
   4 *offspring* – *children* (too formal)
   5 *consuming* – *eating* (too formal)
   6 *came across* – this is marginal: some people might prefer *discovered*
   7 *thing* – some people might prefer *object*
   8 *pretty* – *rather* (too informal)
   9 *stuff* – *products* (too informal)
   10 *put* – *enclosed* (too informal)
   11 *assist* – *help* (maybe too formal?)
   12 *thus* – *therefore/so* (too formal?)
   13 *a re-occurrence of the problem* – *the problem happening/occurring again* (again marginal – some people would find the original acceptable)
   14 *confident* – *sure* (too formal)
   15 *re-imbursement* – *refund* (too formal)
   16 *just right* – *appropriate* (too informal)
   17 *forthwith* – *as soon as possible* (too formal/old-fashioned)
   18 *Best wishes* – *Yours faithfully* (standard ending to a formal letter if you have put *Dear Sir/Madam*)

10.7 Hearing perception

Aim and procedure

See Introduction.

Tapescript

(* = tone)

well, anyway, I was out with the kids
* y'know, took 'em for a walk *y'know, like, in the buggy * and they was howling for something to eat *so we moseys into the corner shop *y'know in Wood Green *and they're starving, y'know *so we get these Supahoops off the shelves *y'know, 33p each *daylight robbery *and well we get out of the shop *and the little nippers just rip open the bag *and then the girl starts screaming *'Daddy, Daddy! there's yucky yucky.'*

10.8 Review

Aim

To review selected language items from Unit 9.

Procedure

Ask students to do the task individually and then compare answers in pairs. If they have doubts, allow them to refer back to the previous unit. Check answers through open-class feedback.

Key
Across
1 co-educational school
2 playschool
3 cause and effect
4 single-sex
Down
1 undergraduate
2 scientific jargon
3 magnifying glass
4 hands-on
5 higher education
6 misconception

11

Living in the city

(11.1) ## To start you thinking

Aim

To introduce students to the theme of the unit through personalisation and discussion.

Procedure

Get open-class feedback from the different groups. For question 3, create two columns on your board to list all the pleasant and unpleasant things about a city.

(11.2) ## Reading

Aim

To practise skimming and scanning.
To practise reading texts in detail.

Procedure

a For all three questions, we suggest the students answer the questions individually at first, and then compare in pairs.

b Set a time limit for this exercise. Pre-teach *rhyme scheme*. Students work individually, then compare answers in pairs.

Key

a 1 1, 2,3 and 4 talk about particular cities, 5 and 6 about cities in general.

2 1 Cairo 2 London 3 Barcelona 4 London

3 **Text 1.** *travel writing in a newspaper*. Features: it is written primarily in the present tense; it attempts to present the scenes as if the reader were actually looking at them; yet the vocabulary is too rich to be a travel guide. Equally possible would be *a history of a city*. In fact, it comes from an article in the *Guardian* by Jan Morris.

Text 2. *a lyrical description*. Features: the poem is in sonnet form; the word order is twisted to fit the rhymes and lines ('I never saw…' becomes 'Ne'er saw I…'); the vocabulary includes items which would probably not be found in prose; there is a use of metaphor (the beauty of the morning is compared to a garment) and personification (the sun is 'he', as is the river; the houses are asleep). The sonnet is by William Wordsworth.

Text 3. *a history of a city*. Features: the piece presents the link between the three 'cities' and their historical development; the style is relatively formal, though the vocabulary is sufficiently rich for it to be travel writing too. It comes from a book called *Barcelona* by Robert Hughes.

Text 4. *memories of a city childhood*. This is in fact a newspaper interview with a British TV personality about her childhood and life in a part of London called Chelsea. Features: the style is relatively informal: the use of the word 'you' to mean 'everybody'; the dialogue is included as direct speech; some of the vocabulary like 'proper flats', 'not much…' 'a decent restaurant', 'bump into', 'lovely'.

Text 5. *a book about town planning*. That it is a book, rather than an article, is shown by the reference to Chapter 1; the vocabulary tends to the academic/ formal ('a profound change'; 'a major feature'; 'a radical construction'; 'acted to bring about…'). The style (long, relatively complicated sentences, including subordinate clauses; multiple use of the semi-colon) is formal.

Text 6. *a social history book*. The features of the piece are somewhat contradictory: on the one hand, it has a rather academic feel, especially the first sentence, which could come from a book about town-planning; however, later in the piece, the writer uses the first person 'I' which suggests a more relaxed, less formal style, as does the pejorative vocabulary like 'soulless' or 'unsympathetic'. The piece comes from a book called *Made in America* by Bill Bryson.

11.3 Vocabulary

Aim

To sensitise students to the connotative power
of vocabulary and to help them think more
creatively about vocabulary use, particularly in
writing.

Procedure

a Write the following phrases on the board:

a simple dress

a simple fracture

a simple-minded person

Elicit from students that 'simple' has different
connotations in the different examples above
(positive, neutral and negative). Ask students
to supply more examples, e.g. 'poor' (a poor
family vs. a poor excuse); 'fat' (a fat child vs. a
fat cheque); 'hot' (a hot temper vs. a hot day
vs. hot stuff).

Make sure all the students can find the
adjectives in the texts, by underlining or
highlighting. Give them a few minutes to do
so. Then put them in pairs and ask them to
decide what connotation the adjectives have
in each case. When they have finished, get
some open-class feedback to check answers.
Make sure you feed back on part a before
going on to b and c.

b Ask students to work individually and
compare and discuss answers in pairs. Go
round the class to monitor and get some
open-class feedback.

c As with b above.

Key

a Text 1: *tangled* positive, *resilient* positive,
tremendous positive, *magnetic* positive, *sickly*
negative, *ghastly* negative, *compact* positive,
labyrinthine neutral or negative, *commercial*
neutral.

Text 2: *touching* positive, *silent* positive, *deep*
positive.

Text 3: *distinct* neutral, *unplanned* negative,
repetitive neutral, *irregular* neutral, *silky*
positive.

Text 4: *sociable* positive, *individual* neutral,
proper neutral, *suburban* positive, *small*
positive.

Text 5: *profound* neutral, *traditional* neutral,
radical neutral, *industrial* neutral, *suburban*
neutral, *vast* neutral, *weakly-organised* negative,
buccaneer negative.

Text 6: *soulless* negative, *impersonal* negative,
skeletal negative, *substantial* neutral, *anonymous*
negative, *fastest-growing* neutral.

b (suggested answers)

commercial can be used to mean 'likely
to sell in large quantities' especially
for works of art and music recordings: *Their
latest CD is extremely commercial and should sell well.*

individual can mean 'distinctive': *She wears very
individual clothes.*

profound often means 'deep' in a positive
sense: *His is the most profound poetry written since
the war.*

substantial has a positive meaning of 'big' or
'solid': *Tim came into a substantial inheritance when
his grandfather died.* (In the text it simply
means 'big' with no suggestion this is a
good thing.)

fastest-growing is often used in a positive
sense, especially in the commercial/
advertising world: *Microsoft was the fastest-
growing computer company of the 1990s.* (A
neutral adjective in the text.)

traditional often means 'pleasantly like things
which happened in the past': *Bread with that
traditional home-baked taste.* (Used neutrally in
the text to mean 'from before', in contrast
to 'new' later in the sentence.)

c (suggested answers)

repetitive usually means that it repeats
something so much that it becomes
boring: *The music is repetitive and superficial.*

irregular usually means that it does not
behave according to the normal rules: *This
behaviour is highly irregular.*

small may be used negatively: *It was a nice
room, but very small.*

suburban more commonly negative or
derogative, is used to mean uninteresting
or unimaginative: *They're nice people but with
definitely suburban attitudes.*

deep has a negative meaning when used
with a negative noun: *He had a deep gash in his
thigh.*

(11.4) Collocations

Aim

To extend students' vocabulary and show them how dictionaries can be used to develop understanding and use of collocations.
To encourage students to prioritise the vocabulary they wish to learn.

Procedure

a Ask students to do the task individually and then check answers in pairs. Check answers through open-class feedback.

b Put students in pairs (or small groups) with a monolingual dictionary for each pair (or group). Check answers through open-class feedback.

c This task should again be done in pairs or small groups. Check answers through open-class feedback.

d Ask students to do this task individually. Students must decide for themselves which words they find interesting or useful. Give students ten minutes for the task. They may then compare and discuss in pairs. Get some open-class feedback on good strategies and why certain students chose certain words and why others did not.

Key

a a7 b15 c9   d2 e6   f3 g1 h5 i11
j10 k14 l8 m13 n12 o4

NB: *shopping mall* was originally American English but it is used more and more in British English. Some dictionaries class *developing world* as a euphemism i.e. that developing really means underdeveloped.

b 2 immediate 3 office 4 public 5 social
6 ground 7 industrial 8 housing

(11.5) Grammar – Position of adverbs

Aim

Adverbs in general, and particularly their position in sentences, remain a difficult area even for advanced students. This section aims to raise students' awareness of, and provide guidance on:

- different types of adverbs and adverbial phrases.
- common positions for the different types.
- the sequence in which adverbial phrases of place and time occur.

Anticipated problems

- Adverbs form a very broad class of word types, many of which have little in common apart from the label given to them. There are many rules which hold true for some types but not for others. Students should be encouraged to look for families of adverbs like those of frequency, manner, etc. as a way of finding a system in what often appears as chaos.
- Even within the same family, different adverbs often behave differently, and students should try to learn the characteristics of a limited number which they feel will be useful in their own speaking and writing. New ones can be added gradually until a large set can be used accurately.

- Changing the position of certain adverbs can drastically change the meaning of a sentence, and students should be encouraged to pay close attention to any which appear in an unfamiliar position and consider what impact this may have on meaning.
- Adverbs are used differently in different genres for various effects, often in ways which appear to contradict what students may already have learnt. To avoid this becoming demotivating, they should be reassured that they do not need to learn all the rare uses to communicate with a high degree of effectiveness.

Procedure

- Write the target words from the exercise, *always*, *in the 1950s and 1960s*, *actually* and *constantly* on the board and ask students what they have in common. Elicit that they are adverbs and an adverbial.
- Tell them that they are taken from the reading texts earlier in the unit, and direct them to part a.

  a Ask students to work individually, without referring back to the texts, before comparing their answers with a partner.

  Ask students to look at the texts and check their answers.

Ask students to work together in pairs to decide if the adverbs/adverbials can go in other positions in the sentences.

Check the answers as a whole class. If students have any questions, ask them if they can find the answers to them for themselves in the next exercise.

b Write three pairs of adverbs on the board *rarely-sometimes / possibly-probably / beautifully-cleverly*, and ask students what kinds of adverbs they are and what they are called. Elicit that:

— *rarely-sometimes* tell us how often something happens, and are adverbs of frequency.

— *possibly-probably* tell us how certain something is, and are adverbs of certainty.

— *beautifully-cleverly* tell us how something happens, and are adverbs of manner.

Ask students to work together in pairs, or, with weaker classes, in groups of three or four.

Monitor closely, giving clues where necessary.

Check the answers as a whole class and answer any queries on form or meaning, but after checking the set of answers for each question stop and ask students whether the adverbs / adverbials can come at the beginning of the sentence. The answers are indicated in the key by *Note that…*

Key

a Sentences in brackets show other possible positions.

1 This was **always** the principal street of Grand Cairo…

(This **always** was the principal street of Grand Cairo…)

2 … they are the products of unconstrained, unplanned growth **in the 1950s and 1960s**…

(No other position.)

3 Singleton and her friends would **constantly** be in and out of each other's flats and houses.

(Singleton and her friends would be **constantly** in and out of each other's flats and houses.)

(Singleton and her friends would be in and out of each other's flats and houses **constantly**.)

4 …great advances in productivity that **actually** reduced total manufacturing employment…

(No other position.)

b The essential lesson to be learnt is given after each item.

1 Tourists *always / usually / often / never* visit the new shopping mall **often**. *Often* can go at the end.

● **Not all adverbs of frequency behave in the same way.**

● **Note that *usually* and *often* can come at the beginning of the sentence if they are followed by a comma.**

2a The planning officer **has** *probably / possibly / definitely* gone to a council meeting.

b The planning officer *probably / possibly / definitely* **hasn't** gone to a council meeting.

● **Adverbs of certainty come after the first auxiliary in affirmative sentences but before it in negative sentences.**

● **Note that some adverbs of certainty, e.g. *probably* and *possibly* can come at the beginning of the sentence if they are followed by a comma, or at the end of the sentence if they are preceded by a comma.**

3 Attitudes to high-rise housing are *always* changing.

Attitudes to high-rise housing aren't *always* changing. (=sometimes they stay the same for a while.)

Attitudes to high-rise housing are changing *slowly*.

Attitudes to high-rise housing aren't changing *slowly*. (=they're changing quickly or not at all.)

● **Adverbs of manner are usually affected by negatives; adverbs of frequency are not.**

● **Note that some adverbs of manner can come at the beginning of the sentence if they are followed by a comma.**

4a The town *quickly / slowly* developed *quickly / slowly / fast / well*.

b The town *quickly / slowly* developed *quickly / slowly* into a city *quickly / slowly / fast / well*.

c The town *quickly / slowly* developed its industry *quickly / slowly / fast / well*.

Key (cont)

- Adverbs of manner usually come:
  - after intransitive verbs.
  - after an adverbial phrase (except phrases of place or time – see 5 below).
  - after the object.

  Most adverbs of manner, but never *fast, hard, well* or *badly*, can come before an adverbial phrase.

- Note that adverbs of manner can sometimes, for literary effect, be placed at the beginning of the sentence followed by a comma, but students are advised against doing this until they gain greater experience.

5 The anti-road lobby presented its arguments carefully *across the whole region in the 1980s.*

- Adverbial phrases of place or time can come at the end of the sentence, and phrases of place usually come before phrases of time, and both come after adverbs of manner.

- Note that phrases of time can come at the beginning of the sentence, but not phrases of place (except in special constructions involving inversion; see Unit 15).

6a **Only** Frances had seen the planning report. = Nobody else saw it.

Frances had **only** seen the planning report. (= She saw nothing else, or she saw it but didn't read it.)

Frances had seen **only** the planning report. (= She saw nothing else.)

Frances had seen the **only** planning report. (= There was only one report.)

b The committee **secretly** arranged to view the new public statue. (= The arrangement was secret.)

The committee arranged to view the new public statue **secretly**. (= The viewing was secret.)

- Changing the position of an adverb can sometimes change the meaning a great deal.

- Note that some adverbs, e.g. *only*, can come at the beginning of the sentence without commas.

(11.6) Learner training

Aim

To improve the students' ability to search for information about grammar on their own.

Procedure

Start by writing the following five incorrect sentences on the board or overhead projector:

* *We arrived to the station feeling tired and dirty.*

* *Emily's lived here since 10 years.*

* *The French doctors have to train longer than the English ones.*

* *I am used to get up at six in the morning.*

* *How many furnitures are you planning to buy?*

Elicit from the students what the mistakes in these sentences are, and where in a grammar book they would look for information about the problem areas.

(Key: prepositions, Present Perfect or *since/for*, articles, gerund vs. infinitive, countable and uncountable nouns.) Write the answers up on the board or OHP against the correct sentences.

a This section gives further practice. Ask students to find the section number in the index in which they would be likely to find information about these mistakes.

b Whereas section a concentrated on finding **where** the relevant information might be, this concentrates on finding the information itself. Ask the students to work in pairs, underlining the information in the grammar book which tells them whether the sentences are correct or not. You should make sure you feed back to the whole class.

Key

a 1 24 (should be *effect*) 2 14 (should be *red brick house*) 3 26/27 (should be *afterwards*) 4 81 (should be *in*) 5 59 (should be *arisen*)

b 1 Correct (Section A – we use an adverb not an adjective to say how something happened or was done)

2 He played **excellently**. (Section A – we use an adverb not an adjective to say how something was done)

3 I saw her dance **in a lively fashion/manner/way**. (Section B – *lively* is an adjective which already ends in -ly; we use a prepositional phrase with *fashion*, *manner* or *way* instead)

4 Correct (Section B – *friendly* is an adjective, although it might be mistaken for an adverb)

5 Correct (Section E – *good* is an adjective)

6 Open the window **wide**, please. (Section D – this adverb has two correct forms, *wide* and *widely*, each with its own different meaning: *widely* is the incorrect choice of meaning in this context)

7 Correct (Section C – this adverb has two correct forms: *cheap* and *cheaply*)

8 It was an **enormously** boring lecture. (Section A – we use adverbs not adjectives to modify other adjectives, including participle adjectives)

9 Correct (Section A – we use adverbs to modify adjectives)

10 He waved his arms around **in an agitated fashion/manner/way**. (Section B – *agitated* is a participle adjective ending in -ed which doesn't have an adverb form: **agitatedly** does not exist; we use a prepositional phrase with *fashion*, *manner* or *way* instead)

EXTRA COMMUNICATION ACTIVITY MAY BE DONE HERE *(see page 125)*

11.7 Listening

Aim

To practise understanding the main points of an interview.
To revise and extend collocations to do with towns and cities; and ways of storing them.
To pool collocations.

Procedure

a The idea that students should store the vocabulary they have learned in meaningful (to them) and interesting categories was introduced in 1.6. In this case, the categorisation is by 'frequency in my country', but there are numerous other ways of dividing up lists of new words:

- words I like vs. words I don't like vs. words I'm indifferent to
- words I want to use vs. words I need to recognise vs. words I don't need
- words with/without an exact translation in my language, etc.

Some of the vocabulary in this section comes up in the listening comprehension in part c.

b Put students into groups of about four. Pooling between students is one way of extending students' range of collocation. Each group should try to make at least twelve new collocations. Stress that they can use either part of the collocation, i.e. they can write *sports + shop*, *car* etc. or *coach*, *tube* etc. + *station*.

Then start pooling them on the board. At the end, the students should write down all the new ones (for them) in their notebooks.

If you have a class which enjoys competitive games, you can award a point to a group for every collocation that no other group has thought of. This encourages groups to write down more interesting ones.

c Ask the students which of the items in section a would be beneficial to a town, and which not. Ask for reasons.

Suggested Focus Task:

Answer these questions:

F 1 What was the survey about, and who took part in it?

2 Was the conclusion a generally happy one?

Play the tape and get answers to the Focus Task questions. Students should then read the questions in their books. Play the recording a second time. Students, as usual, should compare answers in pairs and small groups before feeding back to the whole class.

Key

b Here is a selective list of collocations:

pedestrian + crossing

traffic + island, warden

bus + driver, stop

housing + conditions, association

sports + car, shop

swimming + club

shopping + street

super + market

public + transport, bar, house, school, convenience

leisure + centre

community + centre

+ road: main road, side road

+ precinct: shopping precinct

+ lights: street lights, Christmas lights, neon lights

+ station: coach station, rail/railway station, train station, tube station, subway station (AmE), police station, petrol station, radio station, television station, naval station

+ park: amusement park, lorry park, science park, theme park, business park

+ centre: town centre, city centre, financial centre, commercial centre, job centre, training centre

+ estate: industrial estate, council estate, real estate (AmE)

+ store: department store, chain store (in AmE virtually any item which in BrE would go with shop, e.g. bookstore, furniture store)

+ library: reference library, children's library, lending library, toy library

+ facilities: sports/sporting facilities, transport facilities

+ shops: virtually any item that can be sold: food shops, book shops, toy shops, coffee shops, sweetshops, betting shops, workshops

+ block: office block, roadblock

c **1** 12 **2** 15 months **3** This one talked to ordinary people, whereas the others depended on experts. **4** That we should stagger working hours to reduce traffic during the rush hours. **5** To isolate the people living outside them. **6** Because it takes you longer to cross it than the time between cars. **7** They use their car to get to the gym in order to take exercise. **8** Old women, young children, people with pushchairs, the disabled... **9** 25% **10** They travel by car, so they do not understand the problems of people who do not have one.

Tapescript

ANNOUNCER: Our guest on the programme today is Neil Le Power, whose book *Town and Around* has just been published. It's a survey of twelve towns and cities in England and Wales, a survey which took place over fifteen months. And Neil is here to discuss the conclusions that the researchers came to. Neil, welcome to the programme.

NEIL LE POWER: Thank you.

ANNOUNCER: Now, we've had endless reports and surveys into British towns over the last few years. What's different about yours?

NEIL LE POWER: Well, I think the main difference is that our report was based on talking to local people. As you say, we've heard many opinions expressed over the last 20 years about the decline of the British town, but these have nearly always been **experts** talking. We talked to ordinary people, over 1,000 in the twelve towns, and we also spoke to more than 300 voluntary organisations. We talked to police officers, local business people, nightclub owners, church leaders, and hundreds of individuals we just encountered in the street, or in the pub, or by arrangement in their homes.

ANNOUNCER: There's a feeling, isn't there, that things have somehow **gone wrong** with British towns. Is that what people told you?

NEIL LE POWER: Yes, broadly speaking, yes. I think we managed to identify three areas where our correspondents felt things had gone wrong or were going wrong. The first of these was the fact that British towns are now dominated by the private car...

ANNOUNCER: Mmm, yes, I thought that was the most interesting part of the book. Because it was a missed opportunity, wasn't it?

NEIL LE POWER: Very much so. A report came out all the way back in 1963 called *Traffic in Towns* which anticipated a lot of the dangers which were threatened by the growth of car ownership, and actually put down several very sensible recommendations, but only some of these were ever acted on. For example, the very simple one that working hours should be staggered to avoid the early morning and early evening traffic jams...

ANNOUNCER: And of course, the infamous ring roads...

NEIL LE POWER: Yes, ring roads have created major psychological barriers to walking or cycling in and out of town centres even from residential areas only ten minutes' walking distance from the centre. In Preston we talked to people living on housing estates only a few minutes' walk away from the town centre who would never dream of walking…there are just too many barriers…pedestrian underpasses, tunnels, steps, broken pavements…

ANNOUNCER: Traffic lights where you have to run like a rabbit to get across in time…

NEIL LE POWER: Well, yes, there's a ring road in Northampton, where it's physically impossible to get across it in less than seven seconds, and yet the traffic is so busy that on average there's only a five second gap between the cars! And if you're a mother with a pushchair, or disabled, it's even worse. No wonder nobody walks! You get the mad situation where people who are going to the gym or the swimming pool to get fit, drive there even if it's just round the corner! In Middlesbrough, a woman told us that people used cars to travel to the next street.

ANNOUNCER: In fact, if you go to the continent, to France, or Germany, you find that city centres have been turned into pedestrian precincts, and the car's been almost banned…

NEIL LE POWER: That's right. And, of course, the person who needs to go by car is often the very person who can't! Like old women and young children. And even though everybody regards shopping as one of the great pleasures…

ANNOUNCER: Surely not!

NEIL LE POWER: …in fact, if you don't have a car, it's a nightmare.

ANNOUNCER: But most people do have a car, don't they?

NEIL LE POWER: Absolutely not. In the survey, we found that three-quarters of housewives in Milton Keynes do not have access to the family car during weekdays. But of course the people who make decisions all drive cars – hardly any of the planners and politicians we visited had recently walked anywhere.

(11.8) Writing – problem, solution, evaluation

Aim

To introduce students to a very common structure for organising argumentative texts in English.
To revise and extend the use of discourse markers.

Procedure

a Ask students to do this activity in pairs. Spend no more than five minutes on it; the important part of it is not so much the ordering itself, as the concentration on the discourse markers.

b The answer to the question is given later in the students' texts, but it is worth asking students to study the three paragraphs without, if possible, looking down the page!

Point out that when we talk about a 'three-phase structure', the length of each phase is flexible: you could have a paragraph (as here), or a page, or a chapter, dealing with each of the three phases.

c This exercise practises the three-phase structure studied in parts a and b.

We suggest that students write their pieces individually, in class or for homework.

When correcting this piece, concentrate on the success with which the students have selected and organised ideas into the three paragraphs and used discourse markers. Give a lower priority to 'local' mistakes such as grammar, spelling, etc. unless your students need specific feedback e.g. for exam purposes.

Key

a Paragraph 1: 9, 2, 6
Paragraph 2: 1, 4, 8
Paragraph 3: 3, 7, 5
The phrases which helped with this are as follows:

– The main reason for **this**… (refers back to **a strange fact**)

– **This** causes two separate problems… (refers back to the parents taking the children to school by car)

– One answer to **both these problems**… (refers back to the problems of traffic jams and declining physical fitness)

– **These** differ from existing… (refers back to **specially designated bicycle paths**)

– In **this** way… (refers back to the fact that these paths are sheltered from roads)

– The advantages of **such** a scheme… (refers back to the idea of building special paths in paragraph 2 and refers forward to the advantage which will be outlined in the remainder of the paragraph)

– …**what is more**… (implies a second or additional item, in fact another advantage to add to the three in the previous sentence)

– A **bargain**… (refers back to the low cost of such paths)

b Paragraph 1: Problem
Paragraph 2: Solution
Paragraph 3: Evaluation

Review

Aim

To review selected language items from
Unit 10.

Procedure

Ask students to do the task individually and then
compare answers in pairs. If they have doubts,
allow them to refer back to the previous unit.
Check answers through open-class feedback.

Key

Across: 1 starving 2 trail 3 minor 4 derelict
5 nick

Down: 1 blaze 2 sneak out 3 vehicle
4 joyrider 5 lad 6 tabloid

Art for art's sake?

To start you thinking

Aim

To introduce students to the theme of the unit by encouraging them to consider how 'narrow' or 'broad' their own and others' view of art is.

Procedure

Give students a few minutes to answer the questions for themselves. Then put them into groups of three or four to discuss their own and others' answers. Get open-class feedback from the different groups. You may like to add views of your own if this seems helpful.

NB: many people have a narrow view of what art is. Ask students which of the following they consider 'art': painting, sketching, sculpture, architecture, music, acting, murals, graffiti, poetry. You may also wish to point out the (increasingly blurred) distinction between 'establishment' art and other forms e.g. 'street' art, experimental art, personal art.

Key

4 The *Mona Lisa* (or *La Gioconda*) by Leonardo da Vinci now in the Louvre Gallery, Paris.

Reading

Aim

To use the ideas in a text to put it in order. To understand the same text in detail.

Procedure

a Use question 6 from section 12.1 to introduce the topic. You might like to write the headline on the board first to encourage prediction.

The gap-filling exercise can be done on the same reading. The two exercises together require quite detailed reading, and should be given plenty of time: students should do it in pairs, and then compare in open class.

b The true/false questions will probably need another reading. This part can be done in pairs again, but ask students to justify their answers with reference to the text.

Key

a (Paragraphs in the right order with missing words.)

  c prescribed; launched; chronic
  e pilot; deprived; social; panic
  a met
  f level
  h huge; low
  b tackle; eligible
  g condition
  d problems; well-being

b 1 T 2 F (taught by artists with no medical training) 3 T 4 F (various economically deprived areas of Manchester) 5 F (the art classes will be free) 6 F (the greatest improvements had been to mental rather than physical well-being) 7 T 8 F (give her Prozac and hope she'll get better) 9 F (annual costs of £10,000) 10 T

Reading

Aim

To practise scanning.

Procedure

As usual, set a time limit for this. In order to give as much practice to as many students as possible, try this variation: put students in groups of three. Ask one student from each group to answer questions 1–5; the second to answer 6–10; and the third to answer 11–15. In any case, insist on support from the text for answers given.

Key

1 British Folk Art (currently on a continuous tour of the country).

2 Two (Awash in Colour and Royal Scottish Academy).

3 Frederic Leighton (Not much fun… basically phoney art).

4 Marlene Dumas (the newspaper and magazine imagery combined with fragments of Old Masters).

5 John Deakin (artists, filmstars, poets, criminals).

6 Jack Yeats (a no-longer neglected visionary).

7 Mark Rothko (But why leave it at that? What is needed is a full comparison of the New York and Cornish artists…).

8 American watercolourists (see Awash in Colour).

9 Alfred Wallis (see British Folk Art).

10 Royal Scottish Academy (extending the invitation to exhibit to young unknowns).

11 Rachel Whiteread (photographs of tower blocks about to be blown up).

12 Depends when 'now' is! (Mark Rothko to 3 Nov is the most likely answer).

13 Duncan Macaskill, Mark Rothko (clear from text) but also Marlene Dumas, Rachel Whiteread, Jasper Johns (from the descriptions of their work).

14 Two (Frederic Leighton & British Folk Art).

15 Jasper Johns (seductive and witty sculptures).

12.4 Vocabulary

Aim

To extend and refine students' vocabulary connected with the topic of the unit and to practise a vocabulary recording technique already presented in the book.

Procedure

a Put students in pairs to complete this task. Pairs may use a monolingual dictionary. Check answers through open-class feedback. Point out that the 'brainmap' is not complete and that they can add to it when they come across new words connected with art.

b Ask students to do the task individually and then check answers in pairs.

Key

a

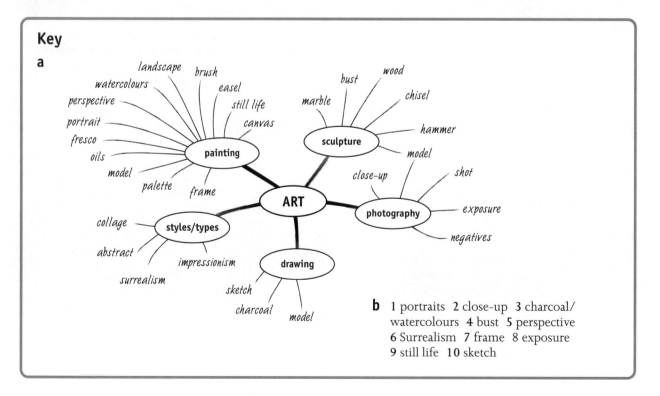

b 1 portraits 2 close-up 3 charcoal/ watercolours 4 bust 5 perspective 6 Surrealism 7 frame 8 exposure 9 still life 10 sketch

12.5 # Grammar – future forms

Aim

This section aims to extend students' knowledge of the range of future forms available in English, and to clarify the differences in meaning and usage. Futures reviewed in Unit 2 are also recycled here in relation to the new forms.

Anticipated problems

- The large number of possible forms used to refer to the future in English can be very confusing to students, and they can easily become demotivated. It is a good strategy to remind them that they already know a number of ways of talking about the future, and that they can extend this knowledge gradually and gently.

- The meaning of many forms depends partly on the mental attitude of the speaker rather than external fact, and this was dealt with in Unit 2. An additional dimension here is the formality of the context.

Procedure

- As this unit recycles future forms used in Unit 2 and adds to them, it would be useful to elicit what future forms they know already and write a list of names and examples on the board. (You could ask them to brainstorm together in pairs for a few minutes before starting the list.)

- You could then ask students to look quickly through Unit 2 again to see if there are any forms they failed to remember, and add these to the list.

a Ask students to work individually before comparing their answers with a partner.

- Check the answers as a whole class and answer any queries on form or meaning.

b For the sentences in this exercise, unusual and improbable contexts could be imagined which would require the use of almost any future form. Although the instructions tell students to think about changes in meaning if different forms are used, ask them to limit their answers to more probable contexts.

- Ask students to work together in pairs, explaining the reasons for their choices.

- Monitor closely pointing out the relevant information and giving clues where necessary. Point out if they have made a wrong choice, but don't give them the correct answer; leave them to think about it together.

- Check the answers as a whole class and answer any queries on form or meaning. If they have more than one answer, have them explain clearly the difference between them. If they miss any of the answers mentioned in the key, you could either elicit these answers or give them and have students explain them.

Key

a a; *be + infinitive*
 a; *be + infinitive*
 b; Present Simple
 d; *be about to + infinitive*

b Less frequently encountered contexts could be imagined which would require the use of other future forms, but the answers below are limited to the more probable contexts:

1 *are you going to do* refers to intentions or plans. *will you do* (less common) simply refers to future facts and sounds rather formal. *are you doing* refers to arrangements already made, which is less likely here given that the question is about *next year*. *leave* refers to a future event determined by a schedule.

2 *'ll be exhibiting* refers to action around a point in time which is emphasised by *this time next week*.

3 *'m having* refers to a pre-arranged plan.

4 *starts* because it is scheduled or timetabled.

5 *is to visit* in news reporting, official notices or formal speech. *is visiting* in informal speech referring to arrangements already made. *will visit* (less likely) is a simple statement of future fact and sounds rather formal. *will be visiting* as a matter of course.

6 *'ll have graduated* is necessary because *by* indicates the event will already be completed.

7 *'m going to drop* is a strong prediction often based on the fact that the action is already beginning, often used as a warning (*be about to drop* is too formal for this context).

8 *is about to demonstrate* refers to the fact that it will happen very soon. *'s going to demonstrate* is possibly too informal and not dramatic enough for the context. *will be demonstrating* as a matter of course.

12.6 Writing – revising and editing written work

Aim

To give students practice in revising and editing their writing.

Procedure

Start by eliciting/revising the notion of students checking and editing their writing before handing it to the teacher. Ask the students to list briefly the kinds of things that a writer should look for when editing/revising. These should be more than just mistakes of spelling and punctuation etc., important though these are. They should also include whether the content and purpose of the writing is appropriate for the intended reader; whether the order of ideas is the best possible; whether material could or should be added or omitted; whether the style is appropriate; whether a piece is clear and easy to follow.

Then ask students in pairs and small groups to read through the piece and edit it. When you are feeding back or correcting, accept any appropriate changes even if they are not exactly the same as in the answer below.

Key

(Mistakes and suggested changes have been circled.)

WILL AUDREY MAKE YOU LOSE YOUR SENSES?

Audrey Walker's new 'experience art room' show is (absolutely marvellous.) Audrey Walker is, in fact, a local girl who (developed)(her present style) over several (years while) she was living in Tokyo.

The show tak(es) place inside one large dark room (with) no windows. (Audrey) describes the show as 'a sensory adventure' and as you enter (X) the room you find out why!(X)

The first sense to be (aff)ected is smell. Inside the room there is a dim blue light but little else is visible. (Then suddenly) you are hit by strange aromas – oranges, ammonia, mown grass, tar, aftershave, burning rubber, roses, wet dog, etc.

Next (X) comes sound. But the sounds don't immediately correspond (to) the smells(, which) don't go away. So you might get birdsong with burning rubber, traffic noise with aftershave, a chainsaw with oranges. (Audrey) says this is where (X) the true (adventure (starts;) you have to make your own connections. And you do start (to) make your own (extremely) (weird) connections.

Then, still in the same blue light, you walk around and touch things (which) are illuminated (dramatically) and draw you to them. Audrey calls this the 'feelie part'. You might touch a tree trunk, while listening to a dentist('s) drill and smelling a strong cheese!

The final stage is (vision). This is achieved with holograms (which) appear in the middle of the room and (are very convincing) because you can walk around them and get a 3-D effect. Your senses are bombarded with contradictions. One I still remember is seeing a spinning sheep('s) head, while touching a pineapple, hearing whal(es) singing and smelling vinegar!

The show is (on) for the next two weeks at the Modern Art Gallery in Bristol Street. It will drive you out (of) your senses. Don't miss it!

(12.7) Listening

Aim

To practise listening to a lecture and extracting detailed information.

Procedure

Use the picture to explain the topic of the listening passage. Explain that all the notes contain some sort of mistake, and point out that the notes are not in the same order as the information on the cassette. Give students time to read through the notes before they listen.

Key

1 Michelangelo Buonarroti (1475–1564).

2 23 years younger than Leonardo da Vinci.

3 'Cinquecento' – 16th century (1500–1599).

4 Worked for Domenico Ghirlandajo for three years.

5 Studied anatomy – dissected dead bodies! Ugh!

6 Michelangelo only interested in human body – Leonardo much more wide-ranging.

7 By 30, Michelangelo considered equal to Leonardo.

8 Probably greatest work = ceiling of Sistine Chapel.

9 Michelangelo worked alone for four years to complete Sistine Chapel fresco.

10 Most famous detail = Creation of Adam.

Tapescript

LECTURER: The second of the two great Florentine artists who make the art of the Italian sixteenth century (or 'Cinquecento') so famous was, of course, Michelangelo Buonarroti (1475–1564). Michelangelo was 23 years younger than Leonardo and outlived him by 45 years. When he was 13 he was apprenticed for three years to the busy workshop of Domenico Ghirlandajo, one of the leading masters of the late fifteenth century. However, Michelangelo did not particularly enjoy his time in this rather traditional workshop – his ideas about art were rather different. Instead of absorbing the facile manner of Ghirlandajo, he went out to study the work of the great masters of the past, Giotto, Donatello and the Greek and Roman sculptors, who knew how to represent every detail of the human body in movement. Like Leonardo, he was not content with learning the laws of anatomy secondhand and made his own research by dissecting bodies and drawing from living models until the human body held no secrets for him. But, unlike Leonardo for whom man was only one of the fascinating puzzles of nature, Michelangelo strove with incredible singleness of purpose to master this one problem as fully as possible. His power of concentration and retentive memory must have been so great that soon there was no posture or movement which he could not draw. By the age of thirty, he was acknowledged as one of the outstanding masters of the age, equal in his way to the genius of Leonardo.

Of course, arguably his greatest work – the ceiling of the Sistine Chapel, commissioned by Pope Julius II – was something Michelangelo tried to evade by saying he was a sculptor not a painter! He started work on a modest design but suddenly changed his mind, shut himself up in the chapel, let no one come near him and started work on a plan which would, as he said, 'amaze the whole world'!

It is very difficult for us to imagine how one human being could achieve what Michelangelo achieved in four years of lonely work on the scaffoldings of the papal chapel. The physical exertion of preparing the scenes in elaborate detail and painting this huge fresco while lying on his back a few inches from the surface of the ceiling and looking upwards all the time is amazing. But this is nothing compared to the intellectual and artistic achievement. The richness of new inventions, the mastery of execution in every detail and, above all, the grandeur of the visions which Michelangelo revealed to those who came after him, have given mankind quite a new idea of the power of genius.

So, let's now look at our first slide, which is probably the most famous detail from the ceiling, 'The Creation of Adam'. Most of us, of course, have seen it so often on postcards, in books, even on CD covers that it is difficult to see it with fresh eyes. But we must try to forget what we know…

12.8 Hearing perception

Aim and procedure

See Introduction.

Tapescript

(* = tone)

It is very difficult for us to imagine *how one human being could achieve what Michelangelo achieved *in four years of lonely work *on the scaffoldings of the papal chapel. *The physical exertion of preparing the scenes in elaborate detail *and painting this huge fresco while lying on his back *a few inches from the surface of the ceiling *and looking upwards all the time is amazing. *But this is nothing *compared to the intellectual and artistic achievement. *The richness of new inventions, *the mastery of execution in every detail *and, above all, the grandeur of the visions *which Michelangelo revealed to those who came after him, *have given mankind quite a new idea *of the power of genius.*

EXTRA COMMUNICATION ACTIVITY MAY BE DONE HERE (see page 125)

12.9 Pronunciation – unstressed endings

Aim

To review how lack of stress leads to weakened sounds, analyse how this works in the case of word endings and improve students' pronunciation.

Procedure

a   Write the words **page**, **encourage** and **camouflage** up on the board. Try to elicit from your students that -age is pronounced differently in each case. Ask your students why they think this is. In most monosyllabic words -age must be stressed (it is the only sound). In polysyllabics when -age occurs at the end of a word it is almost always unstressed and weakens to /ɪdʒ/

○ **O** ○
e.g. encourage

but not always! There are some words which retain a vestigial French pronunciation /aːʒ/ (though not word stress)

O ○ ○
e.g. camouflage

Refer students to the task in their books. Put them into pairs or small groups and check answers through open-class feedback.

b   Put students in teams for this quiz. Play the tape. There is a gap after each beep to allow teams to answer. Pause the tape if your students need more time. Teams score two points for the right answer with the right pronunciation but no points if the pronunciation is incorrect!

c   Write the words **face** and **surface** on the board. Try to elicit from your students that -ace is pronounced differently in the two words. They should now be able to tell you why (-ace in unstressed last position changes from /eɪs/ to either /ɪs/ or /əs/).

Do the same with **rate** and **elaborate**, again eliciting why the -ate changes. This time add **hesitate** and elicit that with -ate a word changes from /eɪt/ to /ət/ but only if the word is a noun or an adjective and not if it is a verb.

Put students in pairs to do this task. Make sure students are clear about the phonetic script they have to use before they start.

d   Get some open-class feedback before playing the tape to check answers.

Key

a

/eɪdʒ/	/ɪdʒ/	/aːʒ/
stage	cottage	massage
rage	marriage	collage
wage	courage	garage (or ɪdʒ)
	cabbage	barrage
	image	dressage
	language	
	garage (or aːʒ)	
	savage	
	sausage	
	carriage	
	heritage	
	bandage	
	postage	

Point out that list two is very long (elicit some more) and list three almost complete as it is!

b   Answers given on tape.

c   1   estimate /estɪmət /;
       estimate /estɪmeɪt /
   2   desperate /despərət /;
       certificate /sɜːtɪfɪkət /
   3   palace /pælɪs /; private /praɪvɪt /
   4   climate / klaɪmɪt /;
       menace / menɪs /

5   terrace /terɪs /; chocolate / tʃɒklət /
6   tolerate /tɒləreɪt /;
    immaculate /ɪmækjulət /
7   preface /prefɪs /;
    accurate /ækjurət /
8   necklace / nekləs /;
    consulate / kɒnsjulət /
9   separate / sepəreɪt / ;
    separate / sepərət /
10 deliberate /dɪlɪbərət /;
    senate /senət /;
    approximately /əprɒksɪmətlɪ /

Tapescript

b 1   Unofficially, English is now the world's second BEEP *language.*

2   A type of food consisting of a long thin tube filled with chopped up meat. BEEP * *sausage*

3   What an athlete might like to receive on a painful muscle. BEEP * *massage*

4   The amount of money it costs to send a letter or a parcel. BEEP * *postage*

5   Journalists often ask politicians or stars a BEEP of questions. * *barrage*

6   A small house in the countryside. BEEP * *cottage*

7   The best place to park your car for the night is in the BEEP * *garage*

8   Another word for rubbish. BEEP * *garbage*

9   The representation of something in picture form, for example. BEEP * *image*

10 Where actors perform in the theatre. BEEP * *stage*

11 What a nurse might put around a cut or other injury. BEEP * *bandage*

12 If there's not enough of something, you could say there's a BEEP * *shortage.*

13 Someone being held prisoner by kidnappers. BEEP * *hostage*

14 In order not to be seen, soldiers need to know how to BEEP themselves. * *camouflage*

15 An amount of money you borrow from a bank or building society to help you buy a house or flat. BEEP * *mortgage*

d 1   Can you give me an estimate of how much it's worth?

    Sorry, madam, it's impossible to estimate something like that until I've seen the piece.

2   He was so desperate to pass the exam that he forged the certificate.

3   Certain rooms in the palace are open to the public but most of them are private.

4   Climate change is going to become a greater menace over the next fifty years.

5   We sat out on the terrace drinking hot chocolate.

6   Susan won't tolerate anything less than immaculate clothing for her children.

7   The preface to the book didn't give a very accurate description of the real situation.

8   June was told to report the theft of her necklace to the consulate.

9   Let's separate the different vegetables and put them into separate pans.

10 There was a deliberate attempt to blow up the Senate building at approximately 11 p.m. yesterday.

(12.10) Review

Aim

To review selected language items from Unit 11.

Procedure

Ask students to do the task individually and then compare answers in pairs. If they have doubts, ask them to refer back to the previous unit. Check answers through open-class feedback.

Key

1   social mix
2   shopping malls
3   inner city
4   labour force
5   ring road
6   traffic calming
7   superstores
8   tower blocks
9   pedestrian precinct
10 multi-storey car park

13

What a good idea!

13.1 To start you thinking

Aim

To introduce students to the theme of the unit through personalisation and discussion.

Procedure

Elicit or pre-teach the meaning of the word *gadget*. If you think your students are unlikely to come up with the names of many gadgets and devices, spend two or three minutes brainstorming for examples first. (Possible ideas: the refrigerator, air conditioning, the aerosol spray, the vacuum cleaner, the camera, the telephone.) Put the students into groups of three or four and set them a time limit to answer the four questions. Get open-class feedback from the different groups at the end.

13.2 Reading

Aim

To predict the content of a text.
To order chronological events within a text.
To interpret a text in detail.

Procedure

a The students should predict the content of the article by answering the five questions.

b This reading should be a very quick one – in order just to get the answers. They should do it individually, with checking done in the whole class.

c Make sure the students understand that the 'correct one' means chronological order, not the order in which the events occur in the article. This part could be done in pairs and small groups.

d Make sure the students have enough time to do this. As a rough guide, allow them one and a half times what it takes you to read it.

Students should do the exercise individually, then compare answers in pairs and groups, then with the whole class. Once again, the reasoning behind the answers is as important as the answers themselves.

Allow students to use dictionaries only for words that are impossible to guess from the context, such as *pad*.

Key

b 1 the ballpoint pen 2 Biro 3 because it was invented by a man called Biro 4 1938 (though a primitive version was invented in 1895) 5 because he didn't patent it

c 9 Primitive version of the ballpoint first invented – 1895

4 Laszlo Biro has idea about a blot-free pen – 1938

7 Biro escapes to Paris – after 1938

1 Biro meets Henry Martin – between 1938 and 1945

10 First Biro factory opens in Britain – during war (1939–45)

6 Launch of rival ballpoint in US – Oct 1945

2 Launch of Biro in Britain – 1946

8 Biros start to sell more than fountain pens – 1950

5 Baron Bich has idea for simplifying plastic pen parts – early 1950s

3 Bic took over their British rivals 1957

d 1 Cheap and trashy.

2 No, it was a luxury purchase.

3 In a pad stuffed down the barrel.

4 That the pen would be more useful if the ink dried quickly.

5 Because he could see a military use for it (the pen was not affected by air pressure, so could easily be used in planes).

6 Almost half.

7 No.

8 He likes the fact that they flow evenly, don't make holes in the paper, are fast, and can be used in the bath. He dislikes the fact that they make people scrawl, make you feel insecure, and can't give you a lovely even movement.

(13.3) Vocabulary

Aim

To increase students' familiarity with multi-word verbs and encourage them to use more.

Procedure

a Pre-teach or elicit the grammatical terms 'main verb' and 'particle'. Ask students to do the task individually and then check answers in pairs. Dictionaries should not be needed. Check answers through open-class feedback.

b Put students into pairs or small groups for this task. Ask them to spend no more than two minutes on each question. Go round the class monitoring.

> **Key**
> **a** 1 try out   2 write off 3 turn into
> 4 date back   5 turn to 6 take over
> 7 dawn on 8 come up with
> 9 get round to 10 bang out
> 11 run out

(13.4) Grammar – multi-word verbs

Aim

Although multi-word verbs, often called *phrasal verbs*, occur in many languages, they are unusually abundant in English. It would be almost impossible to speak English naturally without an ability to use them accurately, and developing that ability is the primary purpose of this section, which aims to do the following:

- consolidate students' understanding of the four grammatical types of multi-word verbs, and provide descriptions of these.

- extend students' vocabulary of multi-word verbs.

- encourage students to use dictionaries not only to check meaning, but as a source of grammatical information.

Anticipated problems

- Students tend to assume that if they recognise the form, they know the meaning. However, there are thousands of multi-word verbs in English and many appear identical but in fact have different meanings and grammar, e.g. *take off* as in *She took off her coat – A stage impressionist takes off famous people – The plane took off.* (Some dictionaries list over a dozen meanings.) Students must look at context very carefully.

- Students tend to focus on the verb and regard the particle as relatively unimportant whereas it in fact changes the meaning drastically.

- Students can become demotivated by the seemingly complex grammar of multi-word verbs, but they should be reassured that there are only four main types given here.

- Students may have encountered 'irregular' multi-word verbs which do not conform to the usual patterns and query these. Assure them that such irregularities are, however, very common.

Procedure

a The aim here is to remind students that multi-word verbs can have one or two particles and that the object can separate verb and particle.

Ask students to work individually before comparing their answers with a partner.

Check the answers as a whole class.

b Ask students to work together in pairs **without** referring back to the Biro text in 13.2.

Monitor closely and point out if they have made a wrong decision as to whether a sentence is right or wrong, but don't correct the wrong ones for them.

Ask students to refer back to the Biro text in 13.2 and check how many they got right.

Check the answers as a whole class and answer any queries on meaning. If students have any questions about grammar, ask them if they can find the answers for themselves in the next exercise.

c Begin by having students read the descriptions, explain any terms which are unfamiliar and give examples.

Ask students to work together in pairs, explaining the reasons for their choices.

Monitor closely pointing out the relevant information and giving clues where necessary.

Check the answers as a whole class and answer any queries on form. (If students query type 4 being generally indivisible, reassure them that there are very few irregular exceptions, e.g. *We should **get the tests over with** as soon as possible –*

where the noun must come after the main verb, unlike type 3.)

Students should be made aware that several verbs have two related forms, e.g. *Our petrol* **ran out** *– We* **ran out** *of petrol.*

d It is a good idea to provide a few spare dictionaries for those students who only have small ones which give inadequate information. Most dictionaries will give grammatical information via abbreviations or symbols, for which there will be a key in the front of the dictionary. Some will give examples of usage which illustrate the grammatical type. This is an opportunity to point out that advanced students really need dictionaries.

Ask students to work together in pairs, explaining the reasons for their choices.

Monitor closely and point out if they have made a wrong choice, but don't give them the answer.

Check the answers as a whole class and answer any queries on form or meaning.

e Ask students to work individually.

Then ask them to compare their answers with a partner. Tell them to explain their answers to each other by referring back to the descriptions in part c if they disagree.

Check the answers as a whole class.

Key

a
1 before the ink <u>ran out</u>.
2 It <u>dawned on</u> him that…
3 [They] <u>turned</u> a disused aircraft hangar near Reading <u>into</u> a Biro factory…
4 …he also <u>tried out</u> a few other inventions…
5 …he could <u>come up with</u> something a great deal simpler.

b
1 …try **it out**
2 …banging **them out**…
3 Correct
4 …come up **with it** NOW
5 …turn **to the production manager**…
6 Correct

7 …dawned **on me**…
8 Correct
9 Correct
10 Correct
11 Correct

c
1 try out 3
2 bang out 3
3 dates back 1
4 come up with 4
5 turn to 2
6 get round to 4
7 dawned on 2
8 write off 3
9 run out 1
10 turn into 3
11 take over 3

d
2 look out 1
3 go down with 4

4 put on 3
5 go through 2
6 take after 2
7 set off 1
8 get to 2
9 call off 3
10 take out 3

e
1 put him up
2 look out
3 gone down with it
4 put on my goggles/put my goggles on
5 go through them
6 takes after her father
7 set off
8 get to the other side of the world
9 call them off
10 taken them out

EXTRA COMMUNICATION ACTIVITY MAY BE DONE HERE *(see page 126)*

(13.5) ## Pronunciation – nouns from multi-word verbs

Aim

To raise students' awareness of where stress goes and so improve their pronunciation of multi-word verbs and nouns derived from multi-word verbs.

Procedure

a Let students read through the introduction in their books. Do not read out the sentences yourself as this would defeat the object of this exercise. Instruct students to mark the stress on the multi-word verbs/nouns using one main stress bubble. Play the tape twice, allowing students to compare and discuss. Use open-class feedback to check answers.

b Students do this individually and then compare answers in pairs or small groups. Do not check answers yet.

c Play the tape, pausing after each sentence to allow students to correct as necessary. Check answers through open-class feedback.

d Rewind and play the tape. Students listen and repeat, both individually and as a whole group, as you see fit.

Key and tapescript

a The car broke down on the way to the airport.

We had a break-down on the way to the airport.

The plane took off about twenty minutes late.

The times of maximum stress for a pilot are take-off and landing.

c
1 You have to check in at least two hours before the flight.

2 There's an automatic back-up every thirty minutes.

3 The new model has been given the go-ahead.

4 The school is trying to build up a library of CD-ROM material.

5 The fumes were so strong that he blacked out for a few seconds.

6 The accident is a real setback for the US space programme.

7 We decided to print out the document.

8 The company has decided to go ahead with the new project.

9 There was a total black-out all over New York.

10 The pay-out in this week's lottery is £12 million.

11 The computer print-out for the program was over twenty pages.

12 The bad weather will set back our building plans.

13 It is imperative to back up at least once a day.

14 We've discovered a dangerous build-up of gases in the pipes.

15 The new cashpoint machines will only pay out if they recognise your thumbprint.

13.6 ## Collocations

Aim

To extend the students' knowledge of collocations connected with the topic of the unit.

Procedure

Ask students to find the collocations in text 13.2. They can then do the task individually and compare in pairs. Get some open-class feedback to check answers.

Key
1 secret formula   2 weekly wage
3 on business   4 massive sales
5 household name   6 luxury purchase
7 advertising campaign   8 register a patent
9 brand leader

13.7 Writing – improving your style

Aim

To improve the students' writing style.

Procedure

Explain to the class that Orwell was a writer who was always concerned with the effect that language has, and who believed strongly in the best possible writing style. (It might be interesting to show the students an extract of Orwell's own writing, and discuss with them if it obeys his rules!)

If your students enjoy guessing games, you might like to ask them to try to guess Orwell's six rules.

Then ask the students to read through Orwell's six suggestions. Make sure they understand the vocabulary. Then ask them to correct the piece in groups.

> ### Key
> (suggested answer)
>
> All English schoolchildren know that the *sandwich* is named after the Earl of Sandwich, a British aristocrat of the eighteenth century. One evening the Earl was playing cards, as usual, when he suddenly became very hungry. Since he did not want to stop playing, or disturb his companions during the game, he asked the servants to bring him something to eat.
>
> The servant reported back to the Earl that he could find only two slices of bread and a piece of cold meat. 'In that case,' said the Earl, 'please place the meat between the two slices of bread, and bring it to me.'
>
> This new snack became most fashionable in the sophisticated clubs and salons of eighteenth century London, was called a *sandwich* after the Earl, and has remained popular ever since.
>
> We can say that if the Earl had come from Newcastle, we would nowadays be asking for a *ham newcastle* or an *egg newcastle*. Such are the mysteries of language!

13.8 Listening

Aim

To practise listening for gist.

Procedure

a The listening comprehension is quite a difficult one, because ideas are expressed rather indirectly, and the main aim is for the students to understand the **gist** of what the professor is saying. For this reason, the piece needs careful introduction.

Direct the students' attention to the two photos and ask which of the two they would buy. Elicit reasons. Ask them to think of other gadgets and machines which are very complicated to use. The classic example is video recorders, which come up in the interview itself.

This should lead on to a short discussion of why people buy complicated machines, even when they never use all the features.

b

> ### Suggested Focus Task:
>
> Answer these questions:
>
> F The professor doesn't talk about technology in this section.
>
> 1 What **does** he talk about?
> 2 Why?

Give the students plenty of time to read the questions before playing the cassette. You will need to point out that the professor starts talking about travel brochures and hotels in order to illustrate what he is later going to say about machines – the manufacturers are trying to confuse the customers, so that they (the manufacturers) can control what the customers buy.

Play the tape in two separate sections, and allow for discussion of the answers, perhaps in groups first, before feeding back to the whole class.

> ### Key
>
> 1 to confuse you (it would also be correct to say 'to spread the customers between the hotels')   2 at random 3 in order to spread the customers around the different hotels (otherwise they would all choose the best one) 4 the manufacturers try to confuse you, because they can more easily control what you do if you are confused 5 a system where safety is very important (the examples given are an aeroplane cockpit and a nuclear power station) 6 if something goes wrong with a video recorder, you miss your TV programme; if something goes wrong with an aeroplane, it

> crashes **7** you can't afford to laugh about machines being complicated if it endangers life **8** so you can easily blame the user **9** because **(i)** the pilot is often killed **(ii)** if you blame the machine, you have to ground many aircraft, which costs a lot of money

Tapescript

Part 1

ANNOUNCER: Professor Harold Thimbleby is Professor of Computing Research at Middlesex University. He has campaigned for many years to make the gadgets and machines we use less complicated. Here he explains his ideas. He starts by trying to answer the question: why do people want to buy such complicated things?

PROFESSOR: Another thing… coming back to your point that we seem to want to buy these things… the evidence is, they're designed to confuse us so that we appear to want them. That's a fairly subtle point. Let's say there's a tourist company… I'll explain it in terms of tourist companies… it's a bit easier to understand the general idea. You want to go to Costa Del Sol and some hotel… you want a swimming pool, you want to be near the beach, whatever, whatever your criteria are, you've got kids and you want… so on. If you look in any travel brochure about the hotels and resorts, they tell you different things about each hotel. And pretty soon you discover you don't know how to make a decision – and you make a random decision – that's deliberate, because if you chose the best hotel everybody would go to that hotel, so what the travel companies do is they tell you 'This hotel's got a swimming pool,' they tell you 'this hotel's got, you know, access to the beach, this hotel's got children's facilities, this hotel…'. Basically, the point of that is to spread the customers out amongst the different hotels because if everybody went to the best hotel, that hotel couldn't cope and all the others would do nothing. So the purpose of the brochure isn't to help you select a hotel, it's to spread the customers among the hotels that they have on offer. That sort of thing goes on with video recorders. The purpose isn't to give you the features you want, the purpose is to get you into the shop, confuse you so that you can be sold a product on the basis that it's a pound cheaper than a competitor's, or that it's made by a brandname that rings a bell or that, you know, it was at the front of the shop. And those are

all things they know how to control. So as you look at it, you know, why are they making confusing gadgets? Well, because they sell. And they sell because confusing people is an easy way of controlling them.

Part 2

PROFESSOR: I once had hope that safety critical systems would be a way of improving things, like… we can all laugh about a video recorder, you know, at worst you record the wrong programme or whatever, you know, it's just irritating and we certainly laugh about it… but that sort of gadget is also available in, for instance, aeroplane cockpits. Have you seen an aeroplane cockpit? You know, they're covered in knobs, buttons and things… or a nuclear power station, you name it, in a safety critical environment they have gone overboard in gadgets that are rather similar to video recorders… and it's then no longer a joke… it's deadly serious. Um… I've worked with some of these interfaces and in aeroplanes, and though it doesn't help me to say this, my cynical view is: they are designed not to be easy to use, they're designed so that when the plane crashes, the manufacturers can say 'it was the pilot's fault', 'cause of course if you blame the machine then, you know, thousands of aircraft have to be grounded and you know, that's a big economic problem, but if you can blame the user… I mean, I'm certainly being cynical when I put it like this, but if you can blame the user, and if the user's killed himself, so much the easier to blame them, then it's **not** the machine's problem…

(13.9) Hearing perception

Aim and procedure

See Introduction.

Tapescript

(* = tone)

and though it doesn't help me to say this, *my cynical view is *they are designed *not to be easy to use , *they're designed so that when the plane crashes, *the manufacturers can say *'it was the pilot's fault', *'cause of course if you blame the machine *then, you know, *thousands of aircraft have to be grounded *and you know, that's a big economic problem, *but if you can blame the user, *I mean, I'm certainly being cynical when I put it like this, *but if you can blame the user, *and if the user's killed himself, *so much the easier to blame them, *then it's **not** the machine's problem…

(13.10) Learner training

Aim

To increase the students' awareness of the opportunities they may have for finding authentic sources of English, even when they do not live in an English-speaking country. If you feel your students either are already familiar with these sources or have absolutely no chance of getting near them, you should omit this section.

Procedure

NB: before you do this activity, you should do some research yourself into what is available locally for your students. You can then use this information if the students' research produces few answers.

a One way of using the flowchart is to ask the students individually to work their way through it **twice** – once at the beginning, and once after they have done the research.

b Clearly you have to adapt to local conditions in this part. In the UK, part of the aim of the activity is for students to use their own English to find out the information, so you can build some language work in here (e.g. question-forming, polite register). Even abroad, you should encourage students to use their English where they can, e.g. in British Council offices.

If the students complete the research, and find there is nothing available for them, you should think about ways of creating sources of real English, e.g. by starting an English club and inviting speakers or showing English films, starting libraries of English language books. These can happen both within a school, and also as an independent activity.

c The reporting back should be done orally, with each student required to report to the whole class, or to groups within the class. A secretary should be appointed in each group or in the class as a whole to write down the information gathered, and then it can be typed up and distributed to the class and/or school.

d The text will depend upon the age and interests of the class. Here is a (non-exhaustive) list of possibilities:

– wallposter (suitable for younger classes)
– formal report
– tabloid newspaper article
– magazine article (humorous)
– magazine article (serious)
– letter to a friend
– advertisement

(13.11) Review

Aim

To review selected language items from Unit 12.

Procedure

Ask students to do the task individually and then compare answers in pairs. If they have doubts, allow them to refer back to the previous unit. Check answers through open-class feedback.

> **Key**
> 2 h chisel 3 l canvas 4 e watercolour
> 5 b paintbrush 6 k retrospective
> 7 f close-up 8 a frame 9 i negative
> 10 j fresco 11 g art gallery 12 d easel

Working nine to five

14.1 To start you thinking

Aim

To prepare students for the themes of the reading passages in the unit.

Procedure

Give students two or three minutes to do the task individually. Then put them in pairs to compare and discuss their answers. You can then discuss answers in the whole class.

14.2 Reading

Aim

To study the vocabulary in two magazine articles.

Procedure

a Direct the students' attention to the two photos. Elicit speculation about the women's jobs, but don't at this stage tell them what they are.

b Ask the students to read through the extracts and answer the two questions. They should do this in pairs and small groups.

c Give the students a few minutes to check their answers.

d Most of the answers require an understanding of individual lexical items. For this reason, we recommend that students are allowed to use a dictionary. Students should work in pairs.

When you are asking the whole class for answers, use the opportunity to elicit the meanings of the target vocabulary, as listed in the key below.

Key

b 1 one is a personal assistant (PA), the other is a rat-catcher.

2 PA: 1,2,5,6,7,11 (though 1 could be either); rat-catcher: 3,4,8,9,10,12 (though 9 could be either).

d 1 True – the piece says that after two years she was promoted to field biologist.

2 False – only when in the production areas of food factories (the other clothing does not relate to hair).

3 False – she makes a site-plan and labels all the rooms on it.

4 True – quarterly.

5 True – pretty standard.

6 False – 'raw materials' would presumably be food of some kind.

7 True – she deals with it 'on the spot'.

8 True – she 'lays down' poison.

9 False – she 'grabs' a sandwich.

10 True – 'every now and then'.

11 False – she 'switches off' at home.

12 True.

13 False – she 'paid her way through it' (i.e. she worked at the same time in order to be able to afford it).

14 True – she 'looks over' it to 'alert him'.

15 True – the secretary who 'logs' it, plus Susan who 'looks through' it, plus Duncan himself.

16 False – although she says he has an 'open-door policy', she also says she refers callers to other managers.

17 True – he 'confides' in her '100 per cent'.

14.3 Vocabulary

Aim

To extend the students' knowledge of idiomatic phrases connected with the topic of the unit and to encourage their active use.

Procedure

a Ask students to go through the texts and underline or highlight the phrases in the box. Encourage pair/group work and discussion. Each pair or group may use a good monolingual dictionary if necessary. Check answers through open-class feedback.

b Ask students to do the task individually and then check answers in pairs.

c Put students into pairs. Go round and monitor/encourage the active use of the idiomatic phrases.

> **EXTRA COMMUNICATION ACTIVITY MAY BE DONE HERE** *(see page 127)*

> **Key**
>
> **b** 2 open-door policy 3 travel itinerary
> 4 draw up a check-list 5 graduate-recruitment fairs 6 take the minutes
> 7 keeps me up to date 8 took a BSc
> 9 refresher course 10 give a talk
> 11 regular customers 12 promoted to
> 13 carry out an in-depth inspection

(14.4) Grammar – noun combinations

Aim

The aims of this section are to:

- familiarise students with the three basic methods of combining nouns, i.e. possessive/genitive 's, use of constructions with prepositions and compounds, i.e. noun + noun.
- demonstrate the applications and limitations of these three methods.
- develop students' intuitive feel for this area of grammar, which is a necessary skill given the abstruse nature of the rules and many irregularities.

Anticipated problems

- Although there are rules, many of these are difficult to grasp, and details of actual usage are very complex. This is also an area of rapid language change. Students are best advised to take what is presented here as a foundation, but to develop their sensitivity via experience through reading.
- Different languages use different methods, many of which are similar to English compounds, and so a common error is the over-use of compounds.
- Students tend to be unaware of the limitations of the possessive/genitive 's and overuse it because it is convenient.
- Prepositions used to combine nouns are highly dependent on context, and choosing the wrong preposition is a common difficulty.

Procedure

a Ask students to work together in pairs, explaining the reasons for their decisions.

Check the answers as a whole class and answer any queries on form or meaning.

Point out that the methods are often combined. An example from the text is *guests for Sunday lunch*, which you could ask students to describe as they did with the other examples.

b Ask students to work together in groups of three or four.

With weaker classes, you could simply have students match the questions with the jumbled answers on page 160. Stronger classes should be encouraged to answer the questions as best they can, and then use page 160 to check their ideas.

Monitor closely answering any queries on form or meaning.

Check the answers as a whole class, and deal with any remaining questions.

c Ask students to work individually, finding possible errors and underlining them.

Then ask them to compare their underlined items with a partner and work together on the corrections. Tell them to explain their ideas to each other by referring back to the information given in part b.

Monitor closely pointing out the relevant information and giving clues where necessary, but don't give them the answers.

Check the answers as a whole class.

> **Key**
>
> **a** food factories; safety boots = simply noun + noun
> part of the job; briefs for meetings = use of a preposition construction
> Duncan's diary; Susan's day = use of possessive (or 'genitive') 's
>
> **b** 1 h Because we use 's with animals or people but not usually with inanimate objects.
>
> 2 c Because in the first, the chicken has been killed and something is made from it, whereas in the second, it has produced something while still alive.

3 j Because in the first, the time is a general time; in the second it is a particular time.

4 i Because *roadside* is a very common expression and so it has become a single word; *the side of the desk* is not so common and so the single word *deskside* has not developed.

5 g The first means the container with its contents; the second is only a specific kind of container.

6 e *Treetop* is such a common expression that it has become a single word, but usually with expressions with *top, bottom, back, middle,* etc. (when they are <u>nouns not adjectives</u>) we use of.

7 f The first is for dogs in general; the second is food that a particular dog is going to eat.

8 a No.

9 k False. Often you mean this but not always. In many cases the relationship between the two nouns is slightly different;

 – *Peter's fax* would mean that Peter sent the fax; the first noun does something to the second.

 – *a woman's dress* simply means that this kind of dress is used by a woman, not necessarily the possession of a particular woman; the first noun uses the second.

 – *the Board's decision* would mean that the Board decided; the first noun does the second.

10 b Because in the second case, the Minister has or owns the tie, and in this case you can only use the *'s* construction; in the first case, the Minister doesn't own the departure but simply departs, so either construction can be used.

11 d True. You can use the noun + noun construction to say where someone comes from.

c This is a true story told by Simon Bates, a **TV personality** who was well-known in Britain. His first job working in the media had been as a disc jockey on a **music station** in Australia. This must have been in the early 1960s.

Although Bates was a Sydney man, he started working for a small station way out in the outback, where the audience consisted of about 20 **sheep farmers** and about ten million sheep. Most of the time, especially in the **middle of the night**, he was the only person present at the station, and did everything – played the records, read out the adverts for farm equipment and beer, introduced the programmes, washed the **tea cups**, everything. And he was completely alone for hours at a time.

Anyway, one evening, **Bates's programme** was going along as usual, and he had just put a record on the **record player** (no tapes or compact discs in those days!) when he suddenly desperately needed to go to the bathroom. It was actually quite a long record (*Hotel California* by the Eagles), so he decided he had enough time to get to the bathroom and back before the **end of the record**. So off he went, leaving *Hotel California* playing to the wastes of the Australian outback.

But when he came back from the bathroom, he realised that, just after he had gone off, the **needle of the record player** had stuck. So the audience had been hearing the same phrase from the song over and over again for five minutes. Bates sighed, sat back and waited for the angry **phone calls**…

14.5 Collocations

Aim

To extend students' knowledge of collocations related to the topic of the unit and further raise their awareness of how collocations are formed.

Procedure

a Put students into pairs for this task. Advise them to read the definitions first and then try to find the collocation which fits. See if they can complete the task without using a dictionary. Use open-class feedback to check answers.

b Put students into small groups of three or four to pool ideas. Give them no more than fifteen minutes. Use open-class feedback to check answers.

Key

a *trade fair* – a very large show of goods; *customer database* – a collection of information about your clients held on computer; *management trainee* – a person learning to run a company; *staff shortages* – a lack of (good) personnel in a company; *shiftwork* – a system whereby some workers work during the day and others during the night; *sweatshop* – a factory where people are employed in bad conditions for low pay; *workforce* – the men and women employed in a factory; *pay packet* – the wages a person earns; *e-mail address* – the place on a computer where you send electronic communications; *web site* – the place on the internet where a company or person can be contacted for information; *office politics* – activities within a company by which some people try to get an advantage over others; *pension scheme* – a system in which a company and its workers contribute money to provide a pension for ex-employees

b (example answers only)

Column A

shop: *shop steward*

trade: *trademark; trade name; trade gap; trade price; trade route; trade union*

customer: *customer demand; customer satisfaction; customer services*

management: *management course; management decisions; management incompetence; management theory*

staff: *staffroom (especially in a school), staff car park, staff association, staff canteen*

shift: *shiftworkers*

work: *workbench, workbook, workhorse, work house, workload, workman, workplace, workshop, workstation, worktop*

pay: *payday, pay negotiations, payroll, payslip*

office: *office block, office boy*

NB: *shop* in the phrases *shopfloor* or *shop steward* means a place where things are made; in its other meaning (the place where things are sold) it has numerous other collocations e.g. *shop window, shop assistant, shopkeeper,* etc.

Column B

+ site: *building site, main site*

+ scheme: *insurance scheme*

+ floor: *ground floor, factory floor,* etc.

+ shop: *machine shop; paint shop, repair shop,* (also all the collocations where *shop* means store e.g. *bookshop*)

+ address: *company address, home address, work address*

+ politics: *company politics, staffroom politics*

+ fair: *book fair*

+ packet: *wage packet*

+ database: *client database, agent database* (virtually anything a company might want to list on a computer)

+ force: *sales force, market force, police force*

+ trainee: *teacher trainee*

+ work: *homework, housework, freelance work, piecework*

(14.6) Pronunciation – compound words

Aim

To raise students' awareness of where stress goes in compound words and let them practise using them.

Procedure

Start by asking students to brainstorm compound words. Write their suggestions on the board, putting brackets round those they mispronounce but without explaining why!

a Put students in pairs for this task. When they have finished, let them compare with another pair and discuss.

b Now instruct them to listen to the tape and check their answers. Stop after each phrase to allow time for correction. Play the tape twice if necessary. Check answers through open-class feedback. Try to elicit that, as a broad rule (though one that has exceptions), if the first part of the compound word is a noun, the stress is on the first part. If it is an adjective, the stress is on the second part e.g. **newspaper** has the stress on **news**, whereas **daily paper** has the stress on **paper**.

Follow up by getting the students to practise the stress patterns. Put the students in pairs or small groups and ask them to talk about a topic for two minutes. Every time they introduce one of the words here, they give themselves a point. The winner has the most points at the end of two minutes. Go round and monitor pronunciation.

Key

a Stress on first part: *workforce, pay packet, sweatshop, trade fair, tea cup, pension scheme.*

Stress on second part: *loudspeaker, daily paper, current affairs, commercial break, absent-minded, cold-blooded, first-class.*

Key and tapescript

b 1 Let's hope the deal is acceptable to the workforce!

2 I don't think your pay packet will be much affected.

3 We need a big loudspeaker in the corner.

4 It's no good turning the place into a sweatshop.

5 I don't usually read a daily paper unless I'm on a train or something. I'm not that interested in current affairs.

6 The trade fair is the quickest way to meet the largest number of potential customers.

7 When there's a really popular programme on TV, everybody makes a cup of tea during the commercial break, so there's an enormous demand for electricity.

8 My husband's so absent-minded he often uses a tea cup to measure out his cornflakes.

9 A police spokeswoman said it was a case of cold-blooded murder.

10 Employers increasingly see a pension scheme as an attractive extra to offer their staff.

11 The conference itself wasn't very interesting, but the accommodation was first-class.

(14.7) Listening

Aim

To give students practice in extracting the necessary information from a semi-authentic dialogue.

Procedure

Ask the students first to study the pie-chart, and speculate on what it might refer to. (In fact, it is the number of businesses in each region of Great Britain.) They will soon see that the figures are impossible as they stand. The bar-chart shows the percentage of people who work a certain number of hours per week, with the white bars indicating men, and the shaded bars women.

Explain that students must listen to the dialogue and correct any mistakes or omissions on the charts. You might use this opportunity to review both how to say decimals in English (e.g. 'fifteen point one per cent') and some simple vocabulary to do with graphs (e.g. *bar-chart, pie-chart, vertical* and *horizontal axis/axes*).

Key

The corrections which have to be made are as follows:

Pie-chart

1 Ireland should read Northern Ireland

2 North West should read South West and vice versa

3 The figure for Wales should read 5.1, not 15.1

4 The figure for East Midlands should read 6.9 per cent, not 69 per cent

5 The figure for the South East should read 35.0 and not 34.0

6 The title is missing, and should read: 'Share of the United Kingdom's number of businesses'

Bar-chart

7 There should be numbers up the vertical axis – 10, 20, 30, 40, 50, 60

Key (cont)

8 They have only put three of the categories along the horizontal axis – the final five categories should read 35–40, 41–44, 45–48, 49–59 and 60 +

9 The title of the horizontal axis is wrong – should read Hours per week not just Hours

Tapescript

1ST MAN: So, you reckon there's a few mistakes on the charts?

WOMAN: No, not a few, there are several, look, it's a complete mess – didn't anybody check these before they handed them back?

2ND MAN: I think they were checked…

1ST MAN: Well, they are usually…

WOMAN: Oh, don't give me that, it's clear to me that no-one has looked at these.

2ND MAN: What's the problem with them?

WOMAN: Well, let's start with the pie-chart, the one with the number of businesses per region, can you see that?

1ST / 2ND MAN: Yeah, yeah.

WOMAN: Well, first of all, some of the titles of the regions are wrong. If you look at the top left, it says 'Ireland', well it should be 'Northern Ireland' of course. 'Ireland' would just mean the Irish Republic, so read 'Northern Ireland'…

2ND MAN: 'cause that's part of the UK…

WOMAN: Right, thank you, and I think 'North West' and 'South West' have been transposed…

2ND MAN: They've been transposed, have they?

WOMAN: Yeah. The names, I mean. Where it says on your pie-chart 'South West nine point one'…

(**2ND MAN:** South West… oh yeah, and North West there…)

WOMAN: …well that should be 'North West nine point four', and 'South West nine point one'.

2ND MAN: That's what it says, is it?

1ST MAN: No, so hang on, no, so it should be… where it says 'South West nine point one' that should be 'North West'…

WOMAN: That's right.

2ND MAN: Oh, swapped 'em around! Oh, I see!

1ST MAN: Yeah, I see.

2ND MAN: You've got to… oh that's easy to do.

1ST MAN: And there's 'North West nine point four' that should be 'South West'.

WOMAN: That's it, that's it.

2ND MAN: Right, OK. All right?

1ST MAN: Sorry about that.

WOMAN: OK, I've not finished yet. We've got some errors with the figures too. Now in the Wales figure, you've put 15.1 – are you with me? – but the original figure was 5.1, they've put an extra one in there, so correct that… that should be 5.1. And then the East Midlands on the right… now that is ridiculous. It says 69 per cent, that would be more than the South East, they've left out the decimal point, are you with me?

2ND MAN: 'cause the segment looks… it's way too small, innit?

WOMAN: Well it should be 6.9 per cent… put the decimal point in.

2ND MAN: What threw me with that was the East Midlands, I wasn't sure exactly what the area…

WOMAN: Yes, thank you, thank you, and the last one is just a small one, but I want to get it absolutely accurate. The figure for the South East is 35.0, not 34.0… if you could correct that…

2ND MAN: It's one out, it's one out…

1ST MAN: It's one out. 35…

2ND MAN: It all makes a difference, doesn't it?

WOMAN: So it reads 35.0, thank you…

2ND MAN: So, well, I mean, so that's it, then, is it?

WOMAN: Well, I think that's it, no, no, no, no, wait, you forgot the title. Now the title should read 'Share of the United Kingdom's…'

1ST / 2ND MAN: 'United Kingdom's'

WOMAN: Yeah, apostrophe Kingdom's number of businesses, and I want that at the top, please, is that clear?

1ST / 2ND MAN: Number of businesses.

1ST MAN: 'Share of the United Kingdom's Number of Businesses.' Right, OK.

WOMAN: All right, now, moving on to the second chart…

1ST MAN: The bar-chart…

WOMAN: Yes, the bar-chart, the one which has nothing up the vertical axis, why? Well, the zero's there at the bottom, but you need to put 10, 20, 30, 40, etc. all the way up the vertical axis up to 60.

2ND MAN: Next to the little marks?

WOMAN: Yes, where those little marks are. Thank you. So – all the way up to 60.

1ST MAN: Well, I mean, that's not too bad, is it? If that's all that's wrong with it….

WOMAN: Apart from the fact that it makes the graph incomprehensible, no, not bad at all, but we've not finished yet, now, along the horizontal axis, if you look, you've only put the figures for the first three pairs of columns, so we've got 20–24, 25–30, 31–34 but then for some reason best known to yourselves, the rest are missing, why?

1ST MAN: I can't??? honestly…

WOMAN: Could you please now put in 35–40, 41–44, 45–48…

2ND MAN: They're going up in fives, aren't they, all the time?

WOMAN: 49–59, so we're increasing the band there and then the final one, please, sixty plus.

1ST MAN: Yes… what was the last one?

WOMAN: Sixty plus… that means more than sixty. Just do a little plus sign.

1ST MAN: I do know that.

WOMAN: Now and lastly, it says 'Hours' as the title for the horizontal axis, now what is that 'hours'? Per day, per week, per century, what? Be accurate, what is it?

1ST MAN: Well, I think it's… it's per week.

WOMAN: Well, write it in, then.

2ND MAN: Would be, wouldn't it? 'Hours… per week.'

1ST MAN: Right, is that it, d'you think?

WOMAN: Well, I think so, unless you can spot anything else.

1ST MAN: No, it looks fine, I'm very sorry about all these mistakes, it won't happen again.

WOMAN: There might not be an again.

(14.8) Writing – ordering an argument

Aim

To enable students to write a 'for and against' argument using a process writing approach.

Procedure

a The topic here is work, but you may wish to change the topic to suit your class. Some other ideas are:

'It is more important to help criminals than to punish them.'

'Love of money is the root of all evil.'

'Most of the technological developments of the twentieth century have done more harm to humanity than good.'

Start with a brainstorm or discussion. You might like to divide students into two groups, with one group listing the points in favour, and the other the points against.

b If students have not done the previous writing work in sections 2.9, 6.6, 8.8 and 11.8, they may need more guidance:

1 Give the students a list of questions to guide their thinking, for example:

- How many arguments 'for' and 'against' are you going to include?

- Is it better to have all the 'for' arguments and all the 'against' arguments together or separated in some way?

- Would you rather have the 'for' arguments first or second?

- How are you going to include examples?

- How are you going to start and finish the piece?

2 Put these two ways of structuring the text (below) on the board or OHP and ask the students to choose between them.

It is important that the students continue to work in groups in the writing phase.

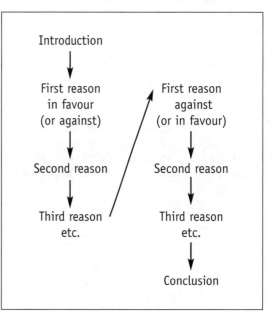

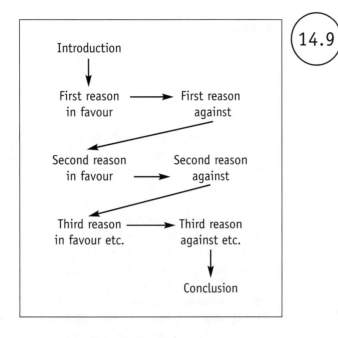

Introduction

First reason in favour → First reason against

Second reason in favour → Second reason against

Third reason in favour etc. → Third reason against etc.

Conclusion

c The main point to make is that the groups are trying to **improve** each other's texts, not just criticise them, and that you are talking about clarity and content, not about the quality or accuracy of the English. The questions in the Student's Book can be used as a starting point.

Students should write on each other's texts in a different-coloured pen.

d It is important that the students now debate the merits or otherwise of the comments from the second group. Whereas students tend to accept a teacher's comments without thinking about them, in this case they have to **evaluate** the comments, and only change the text if they want.

e This is the most important phase, as students have to be prepared to change their original text completely if that is what is required. Give them plenty of time to re-read their texts.

f Only small changes should be made at this point. Let the students decide what is to be done with the finished text. They may like to 'publish' the text in some way – by putting it on a public notice board and asking for comments, printing it in the school magazine, putting it on the school's website and asking for comments. An adventurous class might like to send it to an appropriate publication and see whether they would like to publish it.

14.9 Review

Aim

To review selected language items from Unit 13.

Procedure

Ask students to do the task individually and then compare answers in pairs. If they have doubts, ask them to refer back to the previous unit. Check answers through open-class feedback.

Key

2 got round to   3 went down with
4 came up with   5 dawned on
6 dates back   7 break-down
8 advertising campaign   9 banging out
10 household name

It makes you laugh

15.1 To start you thinking

Aim

To introduce students to the theme of the unit through personal reaction and discussion.

Procedure

a Put students in pairs or groups of three and allow them to react to the cartoons together and discuss which they find funny and which not. Give them no more than three minutes for this. Get some whole class feedback.

b Put students into different small groupings. Refer them to the pictures in the book and check that they know who the characters are. If possible, cut out some pictures from TV listings of local comedy stars/shows to prompt discussion. Give them five minutes to discuss which comedy shows and comedians they know and like. Get some open-class feedback at the end. You may also like to join in.

15.2 Reading

Aim

To predict the content of a text from the headline.
To practise skimming.
To read for detail.

Procedure

a Direct your students' attention to the headline in the Student's Book (or you could write it on the board with books closed). Make sure they do not see the article itself at this stage.

Students write down individually the ten items they predict will appear, and then, in pairs, explain and justify their choices. If you have time, you could ask the pairs to come up with a 'super-list' of, say, 15 items which they compare with the text at the very end (after part c).

b Make sure the students read the three statements before they read the text, and give them a time limit of, say, two minutes.

c Although this is a more detailed reading, avoid using dictionaries at this stage, as some of the vocabulary is dealt with in 15.3. Students should do this section individually at first, then compare answers in pairs or small groups, and then feed back to the whole class.

Key

b 1 False 2 False 3 True

c 1 False 2 False 3 True 4 False 5 False 6 True 7 True 8 True 9 False 10 True

---

15.3 Vocabulary

Aim

To help students understand vocabulary through recognising synonymous expressions.

Procedure

Make sure students understand the task and know that the words come in the same order as in the article. Do the first one in open class as an example. Ask students to do the task individually and then check answers in pairs. Use open-class feedback to check answers.

Key

1 buddy 2 long face 3 misery 4 alter
5 astonishing 6 turn up their noses at
7 outcome 8 garbage 9 trigger
10 die away 11 jump in 12 peak
13 crucial 14 open up 15 'die'

15.4 Collocations

Aim

To extend students' knowledge of collocations related to the unit theme.

Procedure

a Put students into pairs or small groups for this task and encourage discussion and pooling of ideas. They may use dictionaries if in difficulty. Use open-class feedback to check answers.

b Ask students to do the task individually and then check answers in pairs.

Key

a 2 d 3 g 4 i 5 l 6 j 7 b/h 8 e
9 k 10 a 11 h/b 12 c

b 1 punch line 2 laughing stock
3 practical joke 4 wry smile
5 double entendre 6 Black humour
7 belly laugh 8 double act 9 slapstick
10 wisecracks

15.5 Learner training

Aim

To revise ways of storing vocabulary.

Procedure

a Ask the students to study the scale carefully for a few minutes. You may need to explain the significance of the three axes and the positions of the examples. You can guffaw and giggle yourself so that students can hear what you mean! The key shows different answers to the sentence gap-filling.

b This activity requires students either to be inventive or remember true-life humorous situations. If necessary it can be done in groups of three or four. Point out the example and ask students to snigger. When they have thought of their situations and are interacting with the other pair/groups, go round monitoring that they have got the right verb and that they can actually make the right noise!

Key

a

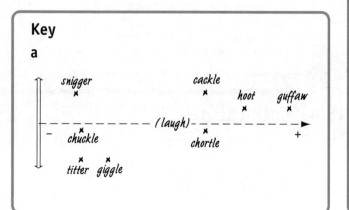

---

1 chuckling/sniggering
2 sniggered/hooted/guffawed
3 chortled/chuckled
4 cackling/sniggering/hooting/ guffawing
5 giggling/tittering

15.6 Reading

Aim

To practise skimming.
To read a text in detail.

Procedure

a Set a time limit of five minutes. Students should work individually, and then compare answers in pairs.

b This requires a more detailed reading. Students should read on their own, then compare answers in small groups.

Key

a 1 False 2 True 3 True

b 1 Because it is a 'specifying characteristic of humanity' – in other words, something that only humans have.

2 The need to 'explain the joke' and, therefore, try to understand what makes us human.

3 In that we use humour to raise questions, criticise arguments with powers stronger than ourselves.

4 They are graffiti artists.

5 To her husband's assassination.

6 So that s/he will eventually be rewarded with laughter.

7 In both circumstances we wilfully allow absurdities and lack of logic or likelihood – we suspend disbelief.

8 There is the *executant*, the joke- or story-teller who establishes the rules and the *respondent*, who goes along with those rules.

9 The listener may be confused or embarrassed if s/he is not sure that what is being said is intended to be humorous.

10 The two points are that there is usually a 'centre of energy' – a word or phrase that the whole joke is based on – and also that the language of humour is often based on double entendres of some type.

**EXTRA COMMUNICATION ACTIVITY
MAY BE DONE HERE** *(see page 127)*

15.7 Grammar – fronting for dramatic effect

Aim

The aim of this section is to introduce students to the idea that English grammar, while not as flexible as the grammar of many languages, does achieve dramatic effects via constructions which place unusual elements at the front/ beginning of the sentence. Two devices are presented and practised: 'inversions' and 'cleft sentences'.

Anticipated problems

- Students often find it difficult to recognise that adverbials are negative and restrictive and consequently require inversions.

- Inversions with initial adverbial clauses containing subject and verb can cause difficulties because students tend to invert these rather than the subject and verb in the main clause, e.g.

  Only after they had arrived at the show did they realise they had forgotten the tickets.

  not * *Only after had they arrived at the show they realised they had forgotten the tickets.*

- Students occasionally overuse cleft sentences when they first learn them, not appreciating that the implied meaning can be confusing to a listener, e.g. *It's a coffee that I want* when ordering coffee implies that there has already been some mistake.

Procedure

a Ask students to rewrite the sentence individually before comparing their answers with a partner.

  - Check the answer as a whole class. Students must have the correct answer before they can do the next task, comparing word order.

  - Ask students to work together comparing word order in pairs. There are several differences as the sentence has been rewritten, but **the important difference is the order of the subject and verb:**

    The whole statement is…

    … is the whole statement

- Have students read the explanation of inversion, check they understand and deal with any problems.

- Write *Simple, Continuous, Perfect* and *Modal* on the board and elicit the auxiliary verbs used for each (Simple = *do*; Continuous = *be*; Perfect = *have*; Modal = *must, can,* etc.), then elicit a question using each form to show students that they are already competent with inversion in questions.

b Have students look at the example before starting the questions and answer any queries on form or meaning.

  Ask students to work together in pairs, and monitor closely giving help where necessary.

  Check the answers as a whole class and answer any queries on form or meaning.

c Ask students to work individually before comparing their answers with a partner.

  Check the answers as a whole class.

  Direct students to the question about style, and if they are unsure, ask which sentence is the least dramatic.

d Have students read the explanation of cleft sentences, check they understand and deal with any problems before moving on to the next exercise.

  Have students look at the examples before starting the questions and answer any queries on form or meaning.

  Ask students to work together in pairs, and monitor closely giving help where necessary.

  Check the answers as a whole class and answer any queries on form or meaning.

Key

a Rewritten sentence:

  The whole statement is 'funny' only if the second outcome is still consistent with the original situation.

  Original sentence:

  Only if the second outcome is still consistent with the original situation <u>is</u> *the whole* **statement** *'funny'.*

  The important difference between the two sentences is the order of the subject and verb as highlighted above.

b 2 Under no circumstances must performers tell racist or sexist jokes.

  3 No sooner had he told one joke than he started telling another.

  4 Not until we had already paid did we realise it was such a tedious performance.

5 Only several hours later did I realise what she meant.

6 Never again shall I attempt to tell a joke when speaking in public.

7 At no time during the show were the performers in any danger.

8 Only in England do people laugh at jokes like that.

9 Hardly had we sat down at our table when the comedian singled out Chris to be the butt of his jokes!

10 Only in Italy can one find the films of the hilariously funny Ugo Fantozzi.

c 1 b 2 c 3 a

Sentence 1 is neutral in style. Sentences 2 and 3 are more dramatic, typically spoken English.

d 3 It's his crazy facial expressions which/that always crack me up.

4 It was my roommate who'd been playing practical jokes on me all along.

5 It's performing to a large audience which/that I absolutely hate.

6 It's our strange sense of humour which/that you're really going to miss.

7 It was puppet shows which/that were always my favourite as a child.

8 It's dirty jokes which/that always get the biggest laughs.

(15.8) Writing – achieving dramatic effect

Aim

To improve students' writing by increasing its dramatic effect.

Procedure

a Go through the 'devices' outlined in the Student's Book and elicit further examples of each type from the students if possible.

Explain that the review in the Student's Book is rather dull, and needs to be made more dramatic. In particular, the underlined sections should be livened up. Do a couple of examples with the whole class.

Ask the students to read through the whole review individually and jot down ideas for making it more dramatic. Then, in pairs, they should write the new, 'dramatic' review.

Feedback can be either in the whole class, by asking for different suggestions for each underlined section, or by asking pairs to exchange scripts with each other and comment, or by taking in the scripts yourself and selecting the best for discussion in a further lesson.

b This task could be set in class or for homework. In either case, ask the students, individually, to note down a few reasons why their favourite author, etc. is so good. Encourage them to use the devices from part a as much as possible.

When correcting this script, you should concentrate on the dramatic power (or otherwise) of the students' English. Other elements such as grammar or spelling should be a lower priority.

Key

(suggested answer)

a Bill Blood's one-man-show is absolutely marvellous/fantastic/brilliant. He stands up night after night and bombards the audience with jokes that have them weeping with laughter and begging him to stop! But what makes him so funny? Is it the funny face, the fast talk or the nervous movements around the stage? According to his manager, Wilbur White, those things are important but the most important of all is timing, timing, timing.

So, remember the name – Bill Blood. He's an absolute scream and he's in town for the next five days, appearing at the Apollo. Under no circumstances must you miss this show!

(15.9) Listening

Aim

To understand and enjoy an extract from a humorous radio programme.
To provoke discussion about what makes us laugh.

Procedure

a Pre-teach the following vocabulary items:
verbatim, overdue, privatisation, the West Country, brewery, hops, banned

> **F**
>
> **Suggested Focus Task:**
>
> Imagine you have just switched on the radio, and have started listening to this programme. Which bits make you laugh and which don't?

b This discussion could work well in either open class, or in small groups, but do not keep it going unless the students are really enthusiastic.

Key

1 That it has an ash-tray. 2 They have probably a) got drunk b) disappeared with the whisky. 3 If they are imports they must come from overseas as well! 4 It is strange for the authorities to worry about the future health of people they are about to execute. 5 The original meaning must be 'it is outside the door of the train'; the second meaning is 'exists' – privatisation leads to cost-cutting so maybe they have decided to save money by removing the platform! 6 For a drink driving offence. Highly implausible – hops by themselves can't get anyone drunk.

Tapescript

PAUL: Lenny.

LENNY: This is from… a letter from Patrick Dixon who says that while at a friend's wedding in Birmingham last week I stayed at the Novis Hotel. The following is transcribed verbatim from the Welcome Pack in the hotel room. 'Non-smoking room. Non-smoking rooms are indicated by a non-smoking sign in the ashtray.'

PAUL: Harry.

HARRY: It's from Lewis's Shipping List. It says: Overdue vessel MV Astra Maris, Asuncion March 16th. Motor Vessel Astra Maris is overdue at Asuncion. She sailed from Buenos Aires on January 18th with a crew of twelve and 22,000 cases of whisky.

I just like the other one that I saw from the *Canberra Morning Star*, which says: 'Traditionally the bulk of Australia's imports have come from overseas.'

PAUL: Well before we start the gripping tie-breaker round, here's a story seen in the *Daily Post*.

RUTH: The anti-smoker international award went to Texas for banning convicts from having a last cigarette before the electric chair. Authorities said it was bad for their health.

PAUL: Alex?

ALEX: Yes, this clipping throws an interesting light on the privatisation of the railways. It's from the timetable of Linx South Central, which operates in the West Country and in the section entitled 'Other Information' there's this advice: 'Before leaving the train, please ensure that the station platform is there.'

PAUL: Yes, very cautious. Harry.

HARRY: Yes. I've got a cutting from the *Chester Mail*, Paul. Conducting his own defence, Mr Rupert Smee said that the house he lived in was a former brewery. 'Is it not possible,' he asked the court, 'that vibration from passing traffic could cause dust from old hops to fall into my tea, making it alcoholic?'

He was fined £200 and banned from driving for six months.

(15.10) Review

Aim

To review selected language items from Unit 14.

Procedure

Ask students to do the task individually and then compare answers in pairs. Check answers through open-class feedback.

Key

1 travel itinerary 2 night-shift
3 refresher courses 4 took … minutes
5 sweatshop 6 draw up a check-list
7 graduate-recruitment 8 shop-floor
9 performance-related 10 pay packet

Communication activities

Unit 1: Defining words

This activity may be done after section 1.6 (LEARNER TRAINING)

Aim

To improve students' ability to paraphrase, define, keep talking.

Procedure

Divide the class into groups of four to six. Each group sits in a circle, preferably with a table in the middle. Give each student a piece of A4 paper, which they should tear into eight equal pieces. They should write one word or lexical item on each piece of paper. These words should not be too obscure: everybody in the class should know them. Then one person in each group takes all the pieces of paper, shuffles them together, and gives them to another group.

Each group now has a pile of about 40 pieces of paper. They should put this pile face down on the table. The youngest person in the group takes the first piece of paper, reads the word to him/herself, and then, **without saying the word itself or showing the piece of paper to anybody**, defines or describes the word to the others. The first person to guess the word wins the piece of paper. Then the person sitting on the left of the youngest person takes the next piece of paper, and defines the word, and so on. The winner is the person who wins the most pieces of paper. If a student picks up a piece of paper, and does not know the word, he/she should put the piece of paper at the bottom of the pack, and take another.

Variation: the teacher decides the 40 words, (perhaps words you would like to revise), writes them on pieces of paper, and gives them to the students. This version takes longer to prepare.

Unit 2: Medical facts and figures

This activity may be done after 2.6 (PRONUNCIATION)

Aim

To practise question forms and expressing numbers, percentages, etc.

Procedure

a Write the following on the board and check that students can SAY them:

101 (one/a hundred <u>and</u> one), 5,625 (five thousand, six hundred and twenty five), 1,000,000 (one/a million), 0.65 (nought point six five), 22.06 (twenty two point oh six), 35% (thirty five per cent), 65.15% (sixty five point one five per cent)

b Put the students into pairs (or A & B teams if you have a very large class). Tell them they must complete the spaces in their factsheets by asking their partners for the information in correct English:

e.g. *Influenza caused .... deaths in 1918.*

The correct question would be: 'How many deaths did influenza cause in 1918?' (Answer: 20 million)

Make sure they understand that they MUST NOT look at their partner's factsheet during the activity. They may do so at the end to check their numbers.

STUDENT A
MEDICAL FACTS & FIGURES

(all figures relate to the UK unless otherwise stated)

.... doctors are currently working in Britain.

The percentage of doctors who are female is 25%.

The country with most hospitals is China, with 63,101.

The highest life expectancy in the world is Japan: .... years for women and 76.3 years for men.

The weight of the male brain is .... grams.

The weight of the female brain is 1,263 grams.

The daily energy need is .... calories for a man and 2,100 calories for a woman.

The commonest blood group is "O+". .... % of the population have it.

The heaviest smokers in the world are the Greeks who smoke .... cigarettes per person per day.

The percentage of smokers who want to give up is 66.6%.

The number of deaths per year caused by smoking is 111,000.

The number of days lost per year due to smoking related illnesses is 50,000,000.

The most popular non-prescription drugs are painkillers, which have annual sales of £ ....

The best selling prescription drug is 'Zantac', with $3,023,000,000 of revenue each year.

The highest number of pills taken by one person in a lifetime is .... , taken by
    C.H.A. Kilner of Zimbabwe between 1926 and 1988.

The longest operation of all time lasted .... hours.

STUDENT B
MEDICAL FACTS & FIGURES

(all figures relate to the UK unless otherwise stated)

155,585 doctors are currently working in Britain.

The percentage of doctors who are female is .... %.

The country with most hospitals is China, with ....

The highest life expectancy in the world is Japan: 83.0 years for women and .... years for men.

The weight of the male brain is 1,408 grams.

The weight of the female brain is .... grams.

The daily energy need is 2,500 calories for a man and .... calories for a woman.

The commonest blood group is "O+". 37.44% of the population have it.

The heaviest smokers in the world are the Greeks who smoke 7.8 cigarettes per person per day.

The percentage of smokers who want to give up is .... %.

The number of deaths per year caused by smoking is ....

The number of days lost per year due to smoking related illnesses is ....

The most popular non-prescription drugs are painkillers, which have annual sales of £195,600,000.

The best selling prescription drug is 'Zantac', with $ .... of revenue each year.

The highest number of pills taken by one person in a lifetime is 565,939, taken by C.H.A. Kilner of Zimbabwe between 1926 and 1988.

The longest operation of all time lasted 96 hours.

Unit 3: Your ideal holiday resort

This activity may be done after 3.8 (LEARNER TRAINING)

Aim

To prioritise factors which go to make up an ideal seaside resort.

Procedure

Put the students into pairs or small groups (no more than four). Explain that their task is to **write** the factors given in order of importance, with the most important first and the least important last. They should also try to think of two more factors to add to the list **before** they start to prioritise.

Possibilities include:

- reliably warm & sunny weather
- easy access e.g. an international airport nearby
- lots of facilities for children
- local people speak English

Compare lists at the end of the activity to see if any groups agree!

YOUR IDEAL SEASIDE RESORT

Put the following factors into YOUR order of importance.

- good selection of shops and markets

- deckchairs and sunshades provided on the beach

- good, inexpensive local restaurants

- proximity to the beach

- good nightlife: bars, discos etc.

- friendly, hospitable local people

- lots of sightseeing potential: countryside and museums, churches etc.

- lots of beach activities: sailing, (wind)surfing, water skiing

- wide choice of accommodation

- chance to interact with local people and get to know their culture

ADD TWO MORE FACTORS TO THIS LIST

- ....

- ....

Unit 4: Crimes and punishments

This activity may be done after 4.8 (VOCABULARY)

Aim

To evaluate the relative seriousness of crimes.

Procedure

Put students in groups of four or five, one of whom must be appointed or elected as secretary. Give each group the list of crimes and possible types of punishments. Their task is to arrive at broad agreement about what punishments suit what crimes. In some cases they must complete the information for themselves e.g. 'imprisonment for ? years'. The secretary must write down the group's conclusions.

When they have finished, either get groups to read out their conclusions and encourage open-class feedback or get them to pass their results on to another group who can write their reactions on the sheet before handing it back.

Warning: this activity can lead to strong disagreements, particularly in the area of capital punishment.

CRIMES AND PUNISHMENTS

- shoplifting (first offence)
- parking illegally
- tax evasion
- murder (after an argument/ planned/serial?)
- vandalism (repeat offence)
- drunken driving
- rape
- kidnapping
- armed robbery
- mugging
- terrorism
- burglary (repeat offence)
- drug trafficking

- a fine
- probationary sentence
- life imprisonment
- imprisonment for ………. years
- community service
- payment of compensation
- the death penalty
- ………………………………………………………………………

© Cambridge University Press 2000

Unit 5: Food and drink quiz

This activity may be done after 5.8 (IDIOMS FROM FOOD AND EATING)

Aim

To discuss and give opinions.

Procedure

Hand out the following quiz. On it you will find 16 facts about food and drink from around the world, some of which are true, and some of which are false. Ask the students to discuss in pairs and small groups, and decide which are which.

Key

1 False – they are just beaten by the Irish, who drink 1,412 cups per head per year. 2 True. 3 False – it is named after the town of Hamburg in Germany. 4 False – but only just. He or she drinks 281 pints per year. 5 True. 6 False. The Finns are the biggest coffee drinkers in the world – 1,857 cups per head per year. 7 True. 8 True. 9 True – in 1985. 10 True. 11 False – the Netherlands, who consume nearly 14 kilos of sweets and chocolate per person per year. 12 False – it should be an egg, not a coconut. 13 False – they are words used for chilli peppers. 14 False – it is the Irish, consuming 3,847 calories per person per day. 15 True. 16 False – it is a kind of frothy sweet served in a glass.

FOOD AND DRINK QUIZ: FACT OR FICTION?

1 The British consume more tea than any other nationality.

2 Chocolate was brought from South America to Spain in the 16th century.

3 The hamburger is so called because it contains ham.

4 Every Czech drinks a pint of beer every day (on average).

5 The first person to chew gum eventually died when he was 102.

6 The Italians drink more coffee than the Finns.

7 14% of the world's population do not get enough to eat.

8 88.5% of an egg is edible.

9 The most expensive bottle of wine sold for £105,000.

10 Perrier water was first produced by an Englishman.

11 The country with the sweetest tooth is Switzerland.

12 You can check if a coconut is fresh by putting it in salty water.

13 The following words: *delicate, mild, medium, warm, piquant, hot, burning, fiery, incendiary, volcanic* all describe types of whisky.

14 The biggest eaters in the world are the Japanese.

15 The Americans eat more vegetables than any other food.

16 A zabaglione is a kind of meat and salad sandwich.

© Cambridge University Press 2000

Unit 6: Financial facts and figures

This activity may be done after 6.6 (WRITING)

Aim

To encourage students to do an 'Information Gap' task by using well-structured question forms.

Procedure

1 The activity must be done in pairs or small teams.

2 **A and B must not look at each other's information sheet!**

3 Each person or team asks questions only where they are lacking information, but must be prepared to answer *Yes* or *No* to questions asked of them.

4 The person (or team) lacking information can only ask Yes/No questions.

   e.g. You can buy a cup of coffee with cruzeiros in ....

   You **can't** ask: *Where can you buy a cup of coffee with cruzeiros?*

   You have to ask something like: *Is it (in) CHILE where you can buy a cup of coffee with cruzeiros? (Answer: No!)*

   OK, is it (in) BRAZIL then? (Answer: Yes. That's right.)

5 If the guesser(s) can't get the answer after three or five attempts (you decide how many), the other(s) can tell them.

STUDENT A
FINANCIAL FACTS & FIGURES

- The insurance company Lloyds of London refuses to undertake only one type of insurance – life insurance.

- The world famous US bullion depository Fort Knox is to be found in the state of ....

- The USA's biggest real estate deal was the 'Louisiana Purchase' from France in 1803.

- .... 's currency, the quetzel, is named after a beautiful bird found in the region.

- Venezuela became the first foreign country to receive US foreign aid in 1812.

- The world's worst rate of inflation was suffered by .... in 1946.

- Argentina had an inflation rate of over 1000% in 1985!

- The world's deepest gold mine is in Carletonville, ...

- China introduced the world's first paper money in 910 AD.

- .... 's currency is considered to be the most difficult to counterfeit.

© Cambridge University Press 2000

STUDENT B
FINANCIAL FACTS & FIGURES

- .... introduced the world's first paper money in 910 AD.

- Guatemala's currency, the quetzel, is named after a beautiful bird found in the region.

- The USA's biggest real estate deal was the 'Louisiana Purchase' from .... in 1803.

- The world's worst rate of inflation was suffered by Hungary in 1946.

- .... became the first foreign country to receive US foreign aid in 1812.

- The world's deepest gold mine is in Carletonville, South Africa.

- Argentina had an inflation rate of over .... % in 1985!

- The world famous US bullion depository Fort Knox is to be found in the state of Kentucky.

- The insurance company Lloyds of London refuses to undertake only one type of insurance – ....

- Japan's currency is considered to be the most difficult to counterfeit.

Unit 7: Are we destroying our own planet?

This activity may be done after 7.6 (WRITING)

Aim

To encourage students to discuss a real world issue with the emphasis on communication and fluency (not accuracy).

Procedure

Set up the debate carefully by:

1 writing the topic for debate clearly on the board ARE WE DESTROYING OUR OWN PLANET? and eliciting a little useful vocabulary;

2 reviewing simple 'discussion language', e.g. I quite agree; You can't be serious; Oh, come off it; Rubbish; Absolutely.

3 appointing a (strong) student as chairperson to run the debate while you monitor and take notes;

4 copying out the following instructions for the chairperson;

5 letting students know you will not be correcting them as they speak or taking part in the debate at all!

During the debate, your role is that of monitor and supporter. Supply vocabulary if students are struggling but **do not correct** their language unless communication totally breaks down.

In your monitoring role, you should note down common mistakes or problems, which can be discussed **after** the debate has been concluded.

CHAIRPERSON

You must introduce the topic for discussion.

'We're here today to discuss … '

Ask people for their opinions.

'What do you think about … ?'

Find out what happens in different countries. (Multinational classes only)

'What's the situation in … ?'

Give everyone the chance to speak.

'Would you like to say something … ?'

Make sure everyone says something (even very shy people).

'We'd like your opinion … '

Don't let one or two people speak too much.

'Thank you. You've made your point.'

Conclude the discussion.

'Thank you all for taking part in this debate. It has been most interesting.'

© Cambridge University Press 2000

Unit 8: Supermarkets – for and against

This activity may be done after section 8.8 (WRITING)

Aim

To practise arguing a point of view.

Procedure

Divide the class into pairs. Give Student A in each pair a copy of worksheet A, and Student B a copy of worksheet B.

Student A should argue in favour of shopping in supermarkets. Student B should argue in favour of shopping in small shops and corner stores. They can add their own arguments to the ones listed on the worksheets. They should also listen carefully to their partner's arguments, and try to think of counterarguments. The pairs must continue for at least ten minutes.

Variation: a strong class could be asked to think up the arguments for themselves (i.e. do not use the worksheets).

WORKSHEET A: ADVANTAGES OF SUPERMARKETS

1   Much cheaper – supermarkets can order goods in greater quantities, so the prices are lower.

2   Saves time – you can do all your shopping in one go, and in one place.

3   Quality is much better – you can trust the levels of hygiene etc.

4   Much more choice – many supermarkets have 15,000 + products

5   More fun – you can meet people and chat in the aisles and queues.

WORKSHEET B: ADVANTAGES OF SMALL SHOPS

1   Personal contact – you have time to chat.

2   Helps build a feeling of community – supermarkets are impersonal.

3   Good for people without cars – supermarkets increase people's dependency on cars.

4   Supermarket food, especially fruit and vegetables, tends to be bland and tasteless.

Unit 9: The difficult student

This activity may be used after 9.9 (LISTENING)

Aim

To practise polite forms of address e.g. explaining, apologising, etc.

Procedure

Divide the class into groups of three. In each group, one student plays the part of the teacher (Bill/Gill Foster), the second student plays a difficult student in the teacher's class (Brenda/ Brian) and the third student plays the mother or father of the student (Mrs/Mr Jones). If you have to have a group of four, the fourth student can play the other parent.

As students are role playing the conversation, go round the class and monitor performance. You should note down common mistakes or problems, which can be discussed AFTER the role play has been concluded.

Give students the following instructions and a role card each:

It is the end of term. It is time for the parent teacher meeting, when parents visit the school to find out about their children's progress.

Role play the conversation between the three/four of you. Try to adopt helpful, non-aggressive positions and come to a compromise and plan of action at the end.

Make sure you are polite at all times.

ROLE CARDS

TEACHER – MRS/MR FOSTER

Unfortunately Brenda/Brian has not had a good term.

Although s/he is clearly very bright, s/he fools about a lot in class, disturbing other students. You try to encourage Brenda/Brian by asking her/him challenging and difficult questions but it seems to make no difference. In addition, s/he is not very good at doing her/his homework and when s/he does it, it has usually been done carelessly and is full of mistakes.

© Cambridge University Press 2000

PARENT(S)

From your point of view, you can't understand the problem. Brenda/Brian is an intelligent and lively child, who is usually obedient, and has many friends both inside and outside the school. But s/he often comes home from school complaining about Mr/Mrs Foster, saying the lessons are too slow. S/he likes Mr/Mrs Foster as a person but the teacher is always dealing with other students, who need more help with their studies than Brenda/Brian. As a result, s/he feels frustrated and misunderstood.

© Cambridge University Press 2000

STUDENT

Your teacher (Mrs/Mr Foster) is not your favourite person. S/he is always asking you the most difficult questions, which sometimes you can answer and sometimes not, whereas s/he asks the other students only easy questions. A lot of the other students are not really interested in learning and are always talking to you and getting you to fool around. You like school but are often bored. You have a lot of other things to do in the evenings (piano lessons, sports practice) so it is very difficult to fit in your homework and you often have to do it on the bus going to school in the morning.

© Cambridge University Press 2000

Unit 10: Eight pictures

This activity may be done after section 10.5 (LISTENING)

Aim

To practise keeping a story going.

Procedure

There are two ways this activity can be organised.

1   Divide the class up into pairs. Student A in each pair receives a copy of worksheet A on page 124. Immediately on receipt of the worksheet (i.e. with no time to think) he or she should tell a story which involves every one of the people or objects. To make sure Student B is listening, ask Student B to re-tell the story back to Student A when he or she has finished. Then reverse the process, with Student B telling a story based on worksheet B on page 124.

2   Student A cuts worksheet A into eight pieces along the dotted lines, and feeds the pieces to Student B one by one, and as Student B receives each new picture, he or she must incorporate the person or object into the story. Then students swap roles and repeat the activity using worksheet B.

WORKSHEET A

WORKSHEET B

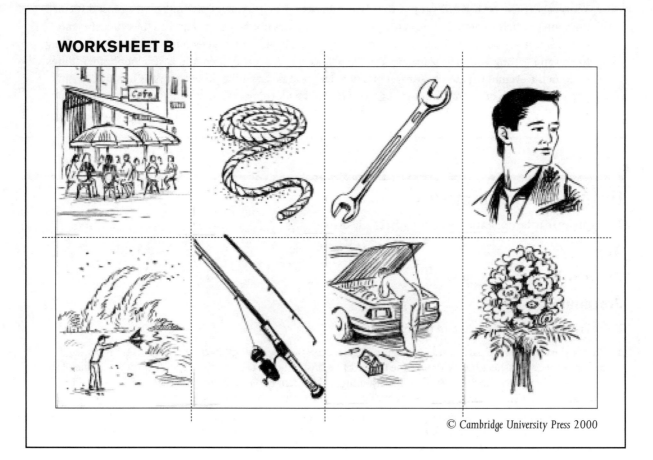

Unit 11: Survey

This activity may be done after section 11.6 (LEARNER TRAINING)

Aim

To practise talking about towns.

Procedure

This will differ according to where the students are studying.

1   If they are studying in an English-speaking country, ask them to go out into the streets of the town where they are staying and interview ten local residents in the streets. They should do this individually, or perhaps in pairs, but not in groups.

Before they do this, they should practise polite requests, such as *Excuse me, I wonder if you'd mind answering a few questions? We're conducting a survey about…* etc.

It is probably a good idea to ask students to write a few questions before they venture out. They could start with a general question such as *What do you like or dislike about X?* but should also prepare a few specific questions like *What do you think of the shopping in X?* They should write down the answers in note form and bring them back to the class.

2   If they are studying in a non-English-speaking country, the street interviews should obviously be conducted in the first language (unless they can find English-speaking residents – they should not, however, interview tourists, who will see the town from a different point of view). Stress the need for politeness, especially if this is the first time they have conducted street interviews.

Warning: In some countries and cultures, it may be difficult or insensitive to conduct street interviews. Consult an experienced local person if you have doubts.

Once they have brought the information back to class, put students together who were not interviewing together. In pairs and small groups, they should draw up a 'consensus sheet', which summarises the responses they have received. A brief oral summary should be given to the rest of the class. This could provide the basis for a wall poster, or piece of written work for homework.

Unit 12: Describing a picture

This activity may be done after 12.8 (HEARING PERCEPTION)

Aim

To practise the language of describing pictures.

Procedure

First check that students are familiar with the language necessary for describing a picture by drawing a frame on the board. As you add the following details (don't worry if you can't draw – students prefer it!), ask **where** they are located:

1   some high mountains *in the background*
2   a log cabin with a chimney *in the foreground on the right*
3   a lake *behind the cabin in the middle of the picture*
4   the sun *above the mountains in the top right-hand corner*
5   a pile of wood *in the foreground in the bottom left-hand corner*
6   a man *beside the wood*

Now check students know how to use the Present Continuous tense when describing what is happening in a picture. Add the following details:

7 the man *is holding* an axe above his head

8 he's *chopping* the wood

9 smoke *is coming*/there's smoke *coming* out of the chimney

As a bit of fun, you could add:

10 a grizzly bear *is running* towards the man!

Now ask your students to take a piece of paper and draw a picture in a frame **without letting anyone else see what they are drawing**. They should not make things too complicated or they won't be able to describe it later. Tell them their picture should contain at least five objects and at least two people or animals doing something interesting or unusual.

When they have finished, put them into pairs. They will need a pencil, an eraser for the numerous alterations they will make, and another blank piece of paper. Student A then 'dictates' their picture to Student B. Student B can ask for repetition or clarification but **must not look** at Student A's picture! When Student B has finished, they can compare the two pictures and discuss differences. Then it is Student B's turn to 'dictate' his/her picture to Student A.

Unit 13: Martian

This activity may be done after 13.4 (GRAMMAR)

Aim

To increase the students' fluency.
To give practice in asking questions and explaining.

Procedure

Divide the class into pairs. Student A should pretend to be a Martian who, strangely, can speak English, but knows nothing about everyday activities and objects. Student B is him or herself.

Student B draws a picture of an everyday gadget or utensil, and should try to explain to the Martian what it is and what it is used for. At any point, the Martian may interrupt and ask for a clarification of some 'new' concept the earthling has introduced. For example:

MARTIAN: What's that?

STUDENT: It's a walkman. I use it to listen to cassettes.

MARTIAN: Cassettes – what are they?

STUDENT: They're tapes where music is recorded.

MARTIAN: I'm sorry – can you explain what 'recorded' means?

Students should take turns to be the Martian.

Variation 1: work with the whole class. One student pretends to be the Martian, and asks all the other students for explanations.

Variation 2: students (in groups) list 6–10 recent inventions, and rank them in order according to criteria such as usefulness, the probable positive or negative effect on our lives, how long they will be with us and how much the students would like to own one. Examples of inventions (at time of writing) might be: mobile telephones, e-mail, CDs, CD-ROMS, video telephones, cloning of animals, genetic engineering of food, virtual reality simulations, cars that can be programmed to take a particular route…

Unit 14: Jobs and personal characteristics

This activity may be done after section 14.3 (VOCABULARY)

Aim

To increase the students' fluency through discussion.

Procedure

Write the following list of personal qualities on the board. Check the students understand what they all are.

- patience
- physical strength
- sense of humour
- manual dexterity
- intelligence
- physical courage
- moral or mental or psychological courage
- good memory
- thick skin (metaphorically)
- creativity

Divide the class into groups of four, and ask them to put the qualities in order of importance for a particular job. Each group should have a different job to discuss. Insist that the four students should come up with a common, agreed order at the end of, say, ten minutes of discussion.

You could ask groups to feed back their results to the whole class, and ask for comments.

Possible jobs to use: dentist, police officer, air steward/stewardess, teacher, novelist, painter, bank manager, supermarket cashier, stand-up comedian, TV newsreader, chef, politician, rat-catcher.

Unit 15: Dictate a joke!

This activity may be used after 15.6 (READING)

Aim

To dictate part of a text as accurately and clearly as possible.

Procedure

Students work in pairs, preferably sitting back to back, or with a physical barrier between them. Each student has a text with half the words and phrases blanked out. Student A has the words that B does not have, and vice versa. By reading aloud, they should complete the text. They are not allowed to look at each other's text until they have finished.

STUDENT A

One day, ... in the park .... a penguin walking by. ...., but he guessed that ...., so he picked it up .... under his arm. .... he saw a policeman .... he should do .... "If I were you," ...., "I'd take him ...."

..............................., the policeman .... through the park, ... the man again, ... still under the man's arm. " .... to take that penguin ...., " he barked. " ....," and he .... So now we're going ...."

STUDENT B

..............................., a man was sitting .... when he saw .... He was a bit surprised, ... the animal was lost, ... and put it .... After a while .... and asked him what .... with the penguin. " ....," said the policeman, " .... to the zoo."

The next day, ... was strolling along ...., when he noticed .... , with the penguin ....

"I thought I told you .... to the zoo," ....

"I did," replied the man, " .... enjoyed it very much. .... to the cinema."